POWERFUL
FEMALE IMMIGRANTS
WHO INSPIRE GREATNESS

VOLUME 3

25 Women Stories Movement

TABLE OF CONTENTS

POWERFUL
FEMALE IMMIGRANTS
WHO INSPIRE GREATNESS

POWERFUL FEMALE IMMIGRANTS

Foreword- By Julie Schaecher

My father immigrated to this country from Mexico in the 1950's. He was one of the oldest of twelve children whose mother had been abandoned by their father leaving them without care. Upon arrival in the US, they slept in a chicken coup and ate meals cooked over an open fire.

Flash forward, I am sitting in the living room of a Nigerian governor's estate where I was invited to stay while I worked as a liaison for their tourism department and the thought running through my mind is, "What in the world happened in our family to take them from a chicken coup to a governor's estate in one generation?" I

It all begins with my grandmother, a powerful female immigrant who refused to believe that living in abject poverty, hoping that the people around her would care for and provide for her and her children was the best she could do. She courageously took her future into her own hands and executed a plan to get her family to America where she believed they had a chance to make a decent life for themselves. Everyone around her told her it was impossible but she believed she could, and so she did.

She would spend her life working in the janitorial department of our local hospital. Along with the help of her three oldest children, my dad being one of them, she was able to provide for her family, buy a home, and ensure that all her children were cared for and loved.

Many of my uncles and aunts grew up to enjoy both personal and professional success. We all marveled when my aunt, the youngest of the twelve, was honored at the White House for being one of Americas distinguished minority businesswomen. It was proof that one woman, making one courageous decision to follow her dreams, can drastically change the future of generations to come.

I remember weeping as I watched my dad cheer for my daughter, his youngest granddaughter, as she received her master's degree in Speech Pathology. He never had the opportunity to finish school and barely had an eighth-grade education but, he had been honored to watch every single one of his grandchildren graduate from college. The pride in his eyes and smile on his face tells the story of how quickly things can turn around. In our family it began with one powerful female immigrant embracing her seemingly impossible dream of a better life.

Michael Butler has assembled an inspiring collection of similar stories from powerful female immigrants who have embraced their God inspired destinies and stepped into their areas of influence with courage and fortitude. These women are making a difference for this generation and for generations to come.

I was recently in a country where women are highly oppressed and often persecuted for even having a desire to go to school. I was there to do a women's leadership conference. One of the young women that I brought with me had just finished speaking from the stage when she was approached by a young lady who had been sitting in the front row. With tears streaming from her eyes she says, "From the time that I was born, I knew that I was called as a leader to the nations. Everyone told me, that it was impossible, but now that I have seen you, I know that I can do it. "

It is important for the voices of the women in this book to be released and for their stories to be told. Their testimonies will ignite hope, light a fire in our hearts and dare us to dream of impossible things.

We now celebrate them and gladly learn from their powerful examples.

Pastor Julie Schaecher

Author, International Speaker, Life Strategies Consultant

Founder of The Now Conference-Global Women's Leadership Movement

Founding Board Member 1040Impact.org

Text: 1040 to
53-555 to donate

INTRODUCTION

Michael D. Butler

For years I've been amazed at immigrants in general and female immigrants in particular. Having traveled to speak in 30 countries I see the passion and the fire in these Powerful Female Immigrants, not just to succeed but to thrive and bring a legacy to future generations.

They are like the women who settled America in the early days as they traveled west in their covered wagons, while the men built saloons and brothels the women started schools and churches. Women, the true nurturers, the women of wisdom like Proverbs 31 speaks of who build several businesses for their family to have multiple income streams as they work from home, guide the house and show their children and their entire neighborhood not just with words but by example, how life can be lived honorably and powerfully.

They go about their daily tasks, rising before sunrise, preparing their kids and their family and their businesses for success. Never seeking recognition or applause, their work is done behind the scenes and in the shadows, when no one is watching. But, yes someone is watching. Someone notices, and we want to honor all of the women in this book with their amazing stories. Their kids rise up and call them blessed.

Women like my mom who threw off the depression of her upbringing in her twenties by finding the truth that set her free and paving the way for generations of Butler's to find hope and walk in the light. She always held my brother and me and my dad to a higher standard. She put something on the inside of us, that something that made you know when things were not quite right and that you couldn't sleep until you made them right.

Special thanks to Liza and Louisa who approached me about doing a book like this a year ago. Their interest and ideas helped me realize it was time and it prompted me to make it happen.

Every one of these Powerful Female Immigrants has a story to share, and it's not just their story that is so compelling but it's what they did when faced with insurmountable odds.

Read their stories, get to know them, follow them on social media and reach out to them. They truly want to help people take action and go to the next level.

I've been able to get to know many of these wonderful ladies personally over the past few years and see them be a blessing to so many in business and in life. We've since gotten together several times and the amazing synergy continues to grow as these amazing women get to know one another, collaborate and plan further ventures together.

Six years ago I learned of a work in the nation of Pakistan that was feeding fifty orphaned children in a safe house. After months of conversations with the team on the ground I decided to make a trip there. When I saw the need and learned the level of care they were providing for these kids not only physically but also mentally and spiritually it made sense for me to start a nonprofit so we could help even more and 1040Impact.org was founded.

Many trips later and taking our board members to see the work firsthand, including two of our authors who let a women's conference, we've been able to expand the work there to rescue dozens more kids, many who had been trafficked and others who had been orphaned or were working as slaves in the brink kiln factory from ages 4-15.

After the US and allied troops pulled out of Afghanistan parents were so desperate they sold their young daughters to traffickers. We were able to intercept, rescue and save many of these girls and the number of children we are now feeding, clothing, educating and ministering to in our safe house and school has grown to 328. We have a full-time team and dedicated staff, many of whom were orphaned themselves are "paying it forward' in their service to help raise and educate a new generation of young people who are self-sufficient and will never be trafficked or slaves again. Our job skills program is helping the young women gain skills in cosmetology and others industries to prepare them for life beyond high school.

One hundred percent of the proceeds from the sale of Powerful Female Immigrants will go to help fund the ongoing work of 1040Impact.org. Your gifts are tax-deductible and can be made online.

Michael D. Butler, CEO

BeyondPublishing.net

Founder 1040Impact.org

Text: 1040 to
53-555 to donate

WALKING FORWARD WEARING MY MOTHER'S SHOES
FROM DINNER HOSTESS TO TV HOST

Migena Agaraj, Albania

The night before my first day of work as a dinner hostess, I could not sleep. It was a night marked by restless anticipation and the weight of the unknown. The minutes seemed to stretch into hours as I lay in bed, my thoughts racing with a mix of excitement and nervousness. It was around 5 AM when my weary mind finally succumbed to exhaustion, granting me a brief respite. Ten minutes, perhaps even less, of fitful slumber. In that fleeting moment, dreams and reality converged, weaving a tapestry of fragmented images. I was happy, I was worried, I was grateful, I was sad, I was it all…

I awoke abruptly, my heart pounding, my eyes wide with panic. The fear of being late for my first day of work on August 27, 2003, surged through me like an electric shock. The world was already stirring to life outside my window, and I couldn't afford to start my new journey on the wrong foot. I could not risk our daily bread. The day was dawning, and the Bronx, with its bustling streets and the distant hum of city life, called out to me. I knew that time was of the essence, that I needed to seize this opportunity that lay ahead. The opportunity to earn, to give, to be, to discover.

In the corner of the room, a white shirt was staring at me. My mother had meticulously ironed it for me. We couldn't afford to buy a new one, but her love and care had transformed it into something more precious than any store-bought garment. It was a symbol of her unwavering love, care, support, and the sacrifices she had made to give me this chance. The chance to continue to be brave, to show up in the world, proud of who I was.

On the couch rested a pair of black pants, a gift from a family friend who had found them for us. These pants had once belonged to a lady whose house our friend looked after. It was an act of kindness, which meant the world to us. They represented the solidarity and generosity of our few friends. I was grateful for them, and my mother was hurting as I wore them. I heard her heart's voice. A child can communicate with a mother's heart and that I did. " I am sorry we cannot buy a pair of brand new pants for you yet. I am sorry I cannot give you more" and tears covered her beautiful face. She began to sob and I held her tight for a few minutes. She felt defeated. This is not how she had envisioned my life in USA.

And then there were my mother's shoes, my favorite part of the uniform. We were fortunate to share the same shoe size, and I had always taken delight in wearing her shoes. They made me feel beautiful, strong, and closer to her. But this time was different. I called them the "survival shoes." They held a special power, giving me the strength to step into the unknown world.

As I slipped into those familiar shoes, I felt a sense of warmth and protection envelop me. They were not just footwear; they were a daily reminder of where I had come from and the journey I had undertaken. "Do not forget where you come from, the steps you took to be where you are," I whispered to myself.

"Honor the shoes, for they will guide you if you listen. They will lead you if you are open."

These were the same shoes my mother had worn for the most part when we were in Albania. They had carried her through the trials and tribulations of life in a distant land, our beautiful Albania and now they were here with me in the Bronx, offering their silent support and strength. Looking back, I don't believe I would be as courageous if it wasn't for my mother's shoes. I would feel lost. Every step I took in them, was a step of love, of a reminder that we would be ok.

With my mother's shoes on my feet and a heart full of gratitude, I set out to face the challenges and opportunities that awaited me on that hot summer day in 2003. From Albania to the Bronx, from sleepless nights to a new beginning, those shoes were a reminder of the strength within me and the love that surrounded me.

The Bronx was a place of new beginnings and unfamiliar challenges. It felt empty, yet very crowded. Strangely, The Bronx did not scare me. I believe the Bronx new the power of my mother's shoes and embraced us. I stepped into my role as a dinner hostess with a mixture of excitement and enthusiasm. I took the 6am bus and traveled to White Plains where the Dinner was. I worked nine hours on my first day and closed the week with three full days. I did not even know how to ask, when pay day was taking place. I could not wait get paid and bring the money home to my mother. The following week, I was handed a paycheck from the owner of the dinner, Bill. I thanked him and was counting the minutes to go home and have my mother open the envelope. $189 dollars. Oh MY GOD. I had never seen so much money in my life at once in my hands, and we earned it. Mom and I together earned very penny.

The days were long, but I was determined to make the most of this opportunity. Earning an income to support my family was fuel for my fire. Working 100 hours a week became the norm. In comparison to how much my family had sacrificed and continued to, the hours I worked felt like seconds. It was a relentless cycle of greeting the customers with a bright smile to their tables, practicing English with them, and ensuring that the guests were happy where they were seated. If I had an iPhone back then, I would have loved to know how many steps I took daily. I walked more than stood. The dinner was busy, all the time and I loved it.

The sleepless nights became a part of my routine. Even after the restaurant closed its doors, my mind would race with thoughts of what the next day would bring. I was driven by ambition and a desire to succeed, and I knew that this job was just the first step on my journey. Time Flew, and my childhood dreams faded with the days.

My mother's shoes were a constant presence, a source of comfort and motivation. They had become more than just footwear; they were a symbol of resilience and a connection to my roots. During the chaotic nights and demanding days, they served as a reminder of where I came from and the path I was forging. I could feel them saying to me: "when will we step into our dreams?" and I kept ignoring them, until 2022...

Television had always held a special place in my heart. It was a medium through which stories could be told, voices could be heard, and dreams could be realized. I yearned to be a part of that world, to share stories that would inspire and connect with others. I remember the six years old Me, holding the hairbrush as a microphone and interviewing imaginary guests on the show, when I was home alone. I asked the questions and answered them (makes me smile each time I revisit the memory).

The journey from a dinner hostess, to cashier, waitress, HR recruiter, Supervisor, Project Manager, Area Director, Director of Business Development to a TV host Associate Producer of "America's Real Deal" was not without its challenges. These are stories for future books as they deserve their own chapters. Rejections became a recurring theme, and self-doubt threatened to derail my aspirations. But my mother's shoes, worn and weathered, held me steady. They reminded me of the strength and determination that had brought me this far.

The transition into television has been a transformative experience. The world of cameras, scripts, and live audiences, a world that demands adaptability and resilience. I embraced the opportunity to connect with people on a larger scale, not only National, but Globally to share stories that resonated with viewers from all walks of life.

As I stood on the set, microphone in hand, I couldn't help but think of the journey that had brought me here. From the Bronx to the television studio in LA, interviewing business owners, multimillionaires and the one and only, Janice Bryant Howroyd, the founder and CEO of ActOne Group. The is path marked by sleepless nights, relentless work, and unwavering determination. My mother's shoes had carried me through it all, a symbol of the strength and resilience that had guided me.

The role of a TV host has allowed me to be a storyteller, a bridge between cultures, and a source of inspiration for others. It is a privilege and a responsibility that I embrace wholeheartedly. My mother's shoes became my companions on this new journey, a silent presence yet the most powerful force that reminded me of the values and lessons instilled in me from a young age.

While my career in television is flourishing, I am exploring other avenues of self-expression. Writing has become a passion, a way to share my journey globally.

During it all, I continue to wear my mother's shoes first before I put on the latest and greatest brands. They are a part of me, a symbol of the journey that had shaped me. I often found myself looking down at them, tracing the scuffs and marks that told our stories.

My mother's shoes were more than just footwear; they were a reminder of the resilience and strength that had carried me through life's challenges. They were a testament to the love and support of my family and the community that had embraced us in our journey from Albania to the Bronx. They were with me, every step of the way. They had witnessed the late nights of studying, skipped meals, the faded rosy face replaced by paleness, the moments of uncertainty. They had become a symbol of adaptability and resilience, a reminder that I could overcome any challenge that came my way.

Becoming a global-focused connector was the natural progression of my journey. I had always believed in the power of connections and collaborations, in the idea that we are stronger when we work together. My mother's shoes were a symbol of unity, a reminder that our roots and experiences connect us to a larger community.

I cultivate relationships and partnerships that transcend borders, fostering unity and understanding in an increasingly interconnected world. My mother's shoes are a reminder that we are all connected, that our journeys are intertwined, and that we have a responsibility to uplift and support one another.

As I stand before audiences as a speaker, CEO, bestselling author, I cannot help but reflect on the significance of my mother's shoes in my life. They had been with me through every chapter of my journey, from Albania to the Bronx and beyond. They were a symbol of resilience, a connection to my roots, and a source of strength. My mother's shoes were my sacred companions throughout this remarkable journey. They were a symbol of resilience, a connection to my roots, and a source of strength.

From the moment I first wore those shoes on that hot summer day in 2003, they became more than just footwear; they became a part of my identity. They reminded me of the sacrifices my family had made, the support of my community, and the values instilled in me by my mother.

As I continue to walk forward in my mother's shoes, I carry with me the lessons of my past and the aspirations of my future. They are a reminder to honor where I come from, to stay true to my roots, and to embrace the opportunities that lie ahead. My journey is a testament to the power of determination, resilience, and the unwavering support of family and community that's ever growing. I am looking forward to connecting with you too, yes! You, the one reading my chapter.

Migena Agaraj

Migena Agaraj is a Global Focused Connector, Business Matchmaker, Founder & CEO of **_Eagles MA LLC_**, a Consulting Firm focusing on Business Solutions. In addition she is an Investor, 10X Certified Business Advisor Mentor and Trainer, TV Host & Associate Producer of **_America's Real Deal_**, Inspirational Global Speaker, Best-Selling Author, Capital Raiser, Passive and Active Investor and a Strategic Partner on a Global Scale.

I was born and raised in Povelce, a small town outside the city of Fier, Albania and moved to New York City in 2003. I live with my parents Isuf and Nadire Agaraj and my brother Arben Agaraj.

I graduated from Hunter College with an Economics Degree, double minored in Italian and History.

Fluent in five languages. Twenty + years of combined experience in Customer Service, Hospitality, Recruiting, HR, Class A Commercial Office Space Real Estate, Business Development, Operations, Client Relations, Capital Raising.

Today, I am the founder and CEO of Eagles MA LLC, a consulting company providing business and real estate solutions, a conduit and business matchmaker. A 3 time bestselling author, "Powerful Female Immigrants Vol 1 & 2", "Real Women in Real Estate", inspirational speaker, 10X business mentor, TV host and associate producer for the investment TV show **_"America's Real Deal"_**. I love to connect, collaborate, and create friendships, partnerships & opportunities on a global scale. I love to read, travel, play golf, host events, cook and enjoy being a guest on Podcasts. In addition, I love hosting Red Carpet

Events. To name a few, "America's Real Deal Red Carpet Premiere", " Michael Blank's Deal Maker Event, etc", panel host "Hero Capital Raising Summit". In addition, I am the Co-Founder of _**"Women In Property Management"**_ Networking Event in NYC. I am also the host of _**"ASKMIGENA SHOW"**_, a podcast streaming on YouTube, LinkedIn, Facebook & Twitter. I am the creator of the Mentorship Program: _**"Migena's 21C's ~**_ The Art of Limited Connecting to Limitless Connections"

Active on all major social medias. Let's connect.

AskMigena.com

PowerfulFemaleImmigrants.com

A MOTHER'S HEART

Nadire Fasko Agaraj, Albania

Representing the Mom's of Immigrants everywhere.

In the world of literature, the power of storytelling knows no boundaries. It transcends borders, languages, and cultures, much like the remarkable journey of immigrant women who have risen above challenges to make their voices heard. In Volume Three of "Powerful Female Immigrants," I find myself privileged to represent the resilient mothers of the daughters who shaped the stories in this volume as well as Volume One and Two, including my daughter Migena Agaraj. She is an author on all three Volumes and other projects.

The Silent Strength of Mothers

Behind every successful author in all three volumes stands an unyielding pillar of strength, love, and sacrifice: the mothers. These unsung heroes have nurtured their daughters' dreams and provided unwavering support, often from afar. They have infused their stories with the essence of resilience, determination, and love, which have become the lifeblood of these powerful narratives. I have had the honor to meet most authors at the book launches and I am touched by their love, kindness, and care towards one another and toward me. I have felt their mother's energies through these women's hugs, trembling voices, painful smiles, and their tears. I have seen them connect with the other women on deep levels. They understand each other, they speak the same language called immigrant. This is not a language taught in schools. You cannot buy a book and learn it, there is no dictionary to translate the words. The immigrant language is learned by living as an immigrant. This is the only way to speak it and understand it. The immigrant language and a mother's heart have this uniqueness in common: You must be one to understand it. I am blessed to be both a mother and an immigrant.

The Creators

I was born in Albania to Sanije and Mustafa. My father divorced my mother when I was five months old. I was taken away from her crib and she was left with a tiny sock assuming some animal had taken me and killed me. This is a story for another time. My paternal grandmother, Pashako, raised me. She is the person I loved the most in the World until I had my children. I learned late in live that in fact she was not my mother. It was so painful; it took my breath away. My love for her, increased by the second. I learned that there is no limit to loving. I was 18 years old when I met my biological mother. My son Arben, in a spitting image of her. I always wondered what a mother's love felt like. When I had my children Arben and Migena, I understood. My mother endured the pain of losing me. She was a beautiful, kind, loyal, caring, loving and so much more woman. I realized how much I missed her presence when I had my own children. No mother and child should ever be separated. I made a promise to myself that I would do everything in my power to always be close to my children.

Roots and Wings

Our authors' mothers hail from diverse backgrounds, each carrying with them the rich tapestry of their native culture. We passed down traditions, language, and values, giving our daughters both roots and wings. We have instilled a deep sense of identity and belonging while encouraging our children to explore the world and chase their dreams. How do I know you may ask? Fair question. Because I am a mother and all mother's hearts beat the same, and they want the same for their children. Also, because my daughter is one of the Powerful Female Immigrants. In addition, because I have seen these women create magic. They are successful doctors, employers, engineers, investors, lawyers. My daughter is friends with them. They build together, they lift each other up. They hold each other accountable. They learn from one another. Powerful Mothers raise Powerful Daughters.

The Sacrifice of Love

In 2003 I became an Albanian immigrant mother.

The sacrifices made by mothers are immeasurable. Many have left behind their homeland, extended families, and familiar comforts. They embark on journeys filled with uncertainty. We face the challenge of adapting to a new culture, often learning a new language, and redefining our roles as women in a foreign land.

Our sacrifices went beyond the tangible. Some of us brought our children here when they were babies. In my case, Migena was a teenager with many unrealized dreams. Dreams she would not share with me. I found out later, she didn't share because she didn't want me to feel guilty for bringing her to a foreign country, away from her family and friends, into the unknown. She was saving me the heartache. Us mothers always wonder if we are enough for our children, if we raised them with everything they need. All I needed as a child was my mother's love and her presence. Her hand on my head would have kept me warm all my life.

Guiding Lights

In the pages of all three volumes, we see how these mothers have been guiding lights, mentors, and role models. We showed our daughters the importance of hard work, determination, and resilience. They exemplified the strength to face adversity with grace and the wisdom to embrace change with an open heart. We instilled in our daughters the value of education beyond the school system, which was often denied, interrupted or not even available to them in their own youth. Mothers work tirelessly to provide opportunities for their children, ensuring they had the chance to excel in their chosen paths. Many have seen their children leave for a better life in the land of opportunities. Many have left their children behind and have fought with all their power to create a better life for their families. I waited 14 years to be united with my son. I know many children who to this day have not seen their parents since they left their countries and vice versa. These unsubscribed pains did not stop us from growing. I see these phenomenal women, who are not only beautiful, but they are strong, successful, caring, giving. Their journeys inspire me. They honor their ancestors. They have not forgotten where they come from.

Immigrant Strengths

Resilience: Us Immigrant women display remarkable resilience in the face of adversity. We overcome significant challenges in our home countries and during the process of migration, this resilience helps us adapt to new environments and thrive despite the obstacles we encounter. We are not afraid to knock on doors and ask for help and most importantly offer help. We can go on for days without sleep, work seven days with no days off and wished there were more days in the week to work some more.

Diversity: Immigrant women bring cultural, linguistic, and experiential diversity to their host countries. This diversity enriches the social and cultural fabric of their new communities, fostering cross-cultural understanding and broadening perspectives. The Powerful Female Immigrants on all three volumes are a great example of diversity starting from external beauty to internal super beauty. We create botanical gardens. We bring diverse loves to the table, different perspectives, wisdom passed on from our ancestors, and not to forget the delicious family recipes.

Family Values and Traditions: Immigrant women prioritize family and community bonds. We maintain strong family connections and support networks, which can be a source of strength and stability as we navigate life in a new country. Us Immigrant women often play a crucial role in preserving and passing down our cultural traditions, including language, cuisine, music, and art. This helps maintain cultural heritage for future generations. All three volumes of Powerful Female Immigrants are filled with breathtaking stories. More need to share theirs. It is one of the highest honors you can pay your ancestors.

Hard Work and Determination: Immigrant women exhibit a strong work ethic and determination. We are willing to put in the effort to build better lives for ourselves and our families, often taking on multiple jobs and pursuing educational opportunities to achieve our goals. My daughter worked three jobs for years. She started college at 24 while having a full-time job. I worked two full time jobs which at first paid $5/Hr. We embraced the challenges and converted them into allies. My Husband was paid $60/day as a construction worker. We were grateful for it all. Grateful for the secondhand mattresses and sheets which were gifted to us. Grateful for the opportunity to work and earn regardless how much we were paid. My son started work the 2nd day he moved to USA. I am so proud of him and his sense of responsibility. He joined us after 14 years of long wait and works harder every day to make up for the lost time. His immigrant spirit fills me with joy.

Adaptability: Immigrant women are skilled at adapting to new environments, customs, and cultures. We are quick learners and open to embracing change, which enables us to integrate into the new societies while preserving our cultural identities. We have respect for education which is often highly valued in immigrant communities, and many immigrant women prioritize the education of their children. We instill a love of learning and emphasize the importance of education as a pathway to success. Not only the education in the school system, but the education in the life system, the best of them all. We learn from others and teach others. We lead by example, we inspire greatness.

Community Building: Immigrant women frequently play key roles in building and sustaining immigrant communities. We establish support networks, organize cultural events, and provide valuable assistance to newcomers, creating a sense of belonging and solidarity. These books are proof.

Entrepreneurship: Immigrant women often exhibit entrepreneurial spirit. They start businesses, contribute to the local economy, and create jobs, showcasing their ability to innovate and thrive as business owners and leaders. The women in these volumes of Powerful Female Immigrants are powerhouses. They are mentors, have multiple successful businesses. They are creators and collaborators; they invest in themselves and others. They own real estate, publish bestselling books and are phenomenal women. You should get to know them too. We the mothers of these women are very proud.

Multilingualism: Many immigrant women are multilingual, which can be an asset in our interconnected world. Our ability to communicate in multiple languages can facilitate cross-cultural understanding and communication. As I mentioned earlier, we also speak the immigrant language. If you are one, please join these women and their journey. Let your friends know they exist. Become part of a global movement and inspire the world one person at a time.

The Proud Legacy

As we celebrate the achievements of our daughters, we also honor the legacy of the mothers, me included. It is a legacy that speaks to the universal power of a mother's love and sacrifice. Through these stories, we recognize that the dreams realized by these immigrant women are not just their own but also a testament to the dreams and sacrifices of their mothers, grandmothers and so on.

In representing all the mothers of the authors, we acknowledge the depth of love, pride, and gratitude that flows through the pages. These mothers are the unsung heroines of the immigrant experience, and their stories are intertwined with the narratives of their daughters.

I dedicate this chapter to the mothers who, through their unwavering support, have nurtured the voices of powerful female immigrants. Their sacrifices and love have empowered their daughters to become the authors of their own lives, and in doing so, they have enriched the world with their stories and their strength. This chapter stands as a tribute to the incredible women who have shaped and continue to shape the course of history through their courage, resilience, and boundless love.

With so much love, and respect for the sacrifices you have made to raise these wonderful women who honor their homelands and USA, I want to thank each one of you for the honor.

Thank you, Michael D. Butler, and Beyond Publishing for this privilege. I feel loved and welcomed and of course younger than ever in the presence of the women.

I wish you all continued success and don't ever stop making us mothers proud.

Sincerely,

Nadire Fasko Agaraj, New York, 2023

Nadire Fasko Agaraj

PowerfulFemaleImmigrants.com

BUSY BODY AND CURIOUS SOUL

Kerry Yu, China

I had just returned from the Miss Universe pageant, where my client had completed a week's worth of grueling competition, testing her on her preparation, skills, and mental toughness at every level. Pushing her mind and being to the limits for the Miss Universe title. I was proud of the work she had put into this moment. This was the path she had chosen, and I was a part of that, helping her compete and win on that stage.

"Kerry is the best mentor anyone could ever dream of having. She has helped me to be who I am today. I am grateful to have her as my manager. I hope her knowledge and experiences will help more people."

Miss Universe Canada 2022
Amelia Tu

For nearly three decades, I have been part of the modeling, fashion, and beauty industry, assisting individuals in realizing their aspiration and objectives. Whether in New York, Milan, or Los

Angeles, the industry has always been characterized by the same desires, dreams, and goals that people set for themselves. Witnessing the miraculous transformation of a young woman stepping into her greatness, discovering her inner lioness, and confidently embracing the present and future she has worked her entire life to prepare for has been an extraordinary experience for me as a coach, mentor, and consultant.

I was once that young girl, growing up wide-eyed and optimistic in China. I recall holding that round globe in my hand for the first time in second grade, memorizing the countries of the world and their locations over the oceans. As I spun the globe in my hand, I could envision all the people from every nation, dreaming, traveling, conversing, and laughing together as one.

I imagined what it would be like in those countries, what the people who lived there were thinking, feeling, and dreaming at that very moment. Were they similar to me? How were they different? Could we become friends and share the stage? Who would be watching?

Finding My Independence at an Early Age

I was fortunate to be raised by parents who let me discover my independence early. They encouraged discovery and exploration, so my brother and I would understand the consequences and rewards of our choices early.

My family sometimes allowed me to figure out things on my own. They didn't make all my decisions for me. I always felt that my parents were smart and brave. When I look back to 70s and 80s, we were fortunate because my parents had good jobs. One thing our family used to do was to have family meetings after dinner. We would sit together, play cards, and then talk about ideas and the future. Those were the best times of my life.

My Love for Travel and How it Shaped My Life

Growing up, my parents believed that education was crucial and provided us with many opportunities to travel around China. From a young age, I was exposed to different cultures and histories, and I soaked it all up like a sponge. These trips were my crash course in education and helped shape my love for travel.

Like many Asian parents, my parents placed a strong emphasis on education for my brother and me. Education provided us choices. I obtained my bachelor's degree at the age of 21 in China before heading to Canada to pursue my passion in the fashion and design industry.

Leaving China for Canada

Leaving China was not a hard time for me; it was a rite of passage where I opened the door to new possibilities. Through my independence, I was able to discover my own identity and how I wanted to relate to the world. Thankfully, my parents were not overly protective, and I was given the chance to learn and grow.

Starting Companies, My Key to Success

I realized early in life that I had a knack for business. I could start a company, create products, find customers, sell those products, and take re-orders before most of my classmates could make it across the street.

The world is a stage, and we are merely actors. From the beginning, I chose to write my own plot, giving me control of the scene and ensuring the outcome of the play. Early on, I found my passion in the business world, and I discovered that it could fuel my dream of creating stages for people all around the globe.

Finding the Right Partners

Finding the right friends, business partners, or soulmate requires wisdom, intuition, and people skills. Although I have not always chosen wisely, I have learned from my mistakes and have always landed on my feet. Having a big picture strategy and balanced expectations can help when making relationship decisions.

Money is Just a Tool

Money is important, but it is only a tool. As a fashion model and a general manager of my company earning a six-figure income at a young age, I have learned that money cannot buy happiness or provide true peace of mind.

My Favorite Job is Being a Mom

Shakespeare said it best: *"All the world's a stage."* I have achieved a great deal, tasting the success of business and financial gain. However, I have come to realize that money is merely a tool and not my purpose. I choose freedom over comfort and value the spotlight but also know when to step away from it. As we progress through different stages of life, we play various roles— sometimes as the main character and sometimes in supporting roles. Regardless of the part I am given, I strive to perform it well.

When my two children were young, I devoted my life to being a stay-at-home mom because my success was not measured by how much money I could make or what kind of material possessions I could acquire. It was measured by what kind of children I could bring into this world. At the end of the day, I believe that there is a difference between what kind of children you could leave to this world and what kind of world you could leave for the children.

Finally Breaking Up

After years of attempting to salvage my marriage, I ultimately concluded that it was in the best interest of both my children's emotional well-being and my own to pursue a divorce. As a result, when my children were aged 10 and 12, I became a single mother with no relatives residing in the United States, no familial support, and no child support payments. Nevertheless, I proudly raised my two children on my own, living in an upscale neighborhood and attending one of the best schools in the state. Rather than viewing myself as a victim, I always believed that everything happens for a reason and was willing to challenge myself to achieve the best possible outcome. I approached this difficult moment in my life with the mindset of "When life gives you lemons, make lemonade." Rather than dwelling on negative emotions, my focus was on finding solutions and improving the situation. In this regard, I find Nike's slogan, "Just do it," particularly inspiring.

The truth is, I'm not a victim; you are not a victim. People who stay stuck in victim mode really don't want success; they just want sympathy. I decided long ago I could settle for sympathy, or I could claim success as my birthright, and I'll take success every time!

Building Character – Finding Courage

Ten years have passed since I was a single mother, and now my children have grown into amazing individuals. My daughter, who is 22 years old, is currently pursuing her graduate studies in psychology. Along with her studies, she also holds two jobs, one as an administrator in her school and the other in a non-profit organization that supports women in need. My son, who is 20 years old, is a talented D1 college football player.

As a parent, I have always strived to be a positive influence on my children. I have taught them to be responsible individuals with a strong sense of purpose towards society. My parents were my role models, and I have become the same for my children.

Now that my children are grown up, I have more free time for myself.. I continue to pursue my passion as a producer and creative director for my shows. I work with fashion designers, models, and I even train pageant girls like Miss Universe Canada Amelia Tu. I have 4 LLCs and a nonprofit,and I love to keep myself busy. I stay curious because that is the secret to staying young.

I firmly believe that life is what you make of it. We should always strive to be happy and take on challenges along the way. Happiness is a state of mind, and it is a choice. We should not be afraid of the unknown, nor of change. Let's embrace life and make the most of every moment.

Creating Influence

I have spent a million or two dollars on plane tickets. I feel like I still have my childhood globe in my hand and that if I fly fast enough, the sun will never set.

Every day, I'm challenged by my children, my students, and my clients to remember that influence isn't measured by the size of your bank account. It is measured by how many lives you touch, how many hearts you inspire, and how many positive changes you create.

So, I urge you to create your own stage, a platform that will endure and make a difference. You probably already know what you stage is. Don't envy someone else's spotlight, embrace your own, nurture it, and let it grow. Invite others to join you, share their talents, and learn from their mistakes. Stages are not meant to be exclusive, but, rather, to be shared, passed on, and amplified. Don't live small; live big, with all your gifts and creativity, and shine a light on others so they can shine, too.

As for me, I'll always be a busy body and a curious soul, with a hunger for new experiences and a thirst for learning.

Kerry Yu

With nearly 30 years of fashion experience as an international model and fashion show producer, Kerry Yu is a seasoned expert in her field.

In the 1990s, she earned numerous modeling awards in Canadian modeling competitions. Since then, she has produced fashion shows and events for over a hundred designers and brands across the globe, including New York Fashion Week, Vancouver Fashion Week, Toronto Fashion

Week, Dubai Fashion Week, China Fashion Week, and China U.S. Fashion Week .

Kerry Yu is the founder of China U.S. Fashion Week and a director of International Modeling and Talent Association in U.S. She manages Miss Universe Canada Amelia Tu, serves as the fashion editor of *Lake Oswego Life/ Style* Magazine and is the CEO of Oceana Blue Productions, LLC.

Currently residing in Oregon, Kerry Yu's expertise and leadership have left an indelible mark on the fashion industry, and she continues to inspire and empower emerging talent around the world.

Kerry Yu can be reached for media, speaking, and interviews at
OceanaBlueUSA.com
PowerfulFemaleImmigrants.com

FROM GEORGIA TO GEORGIA
FINDING PURPOSE AND BUILDING DREAMS

Ana Megrelishvili, Georgia

The story of how I was born is unique due to the fact that I was born on a moving train. My mother was eight months pregnant when she decided she should give birth in her hometown Gori, Georgia and not in Moscow, Russia where she was living. She took a train from Moscow in June of 1988. I was not due for another month, so she thought she was in the clear for travel. The overall trip should have been 3 days long, but she never finished the journey on that particular train. I was too impatient to meet this world and my mother went into labor on the train. The train was in the middle of nowhere and it could not stop. The conductor made an announcement asking for any doctors and nurses to proceed to the train car where my mother was. Surprisingly, there were quite a few on that train. My mother received better medical attention than she would have at the hospital. I was successfully born. When the train arrived at the closest city of Tula, Russia, the ambulance was already waiting for us, and we were taken to the hospital for observation. Three days later, we were discharged from the hospital, and we finally arrived in Gori. I received the nickname, Matarebela, which translates from Georgian language as "born on the train".

When I was fifteen, I heard of a competition in English and went to it without telling my parents. The grand prize was a fully paid trip to the US where I would live for a year as an exchange student. I was the last person in the program to be matched with a host family, but they were the first example of a happily married couple and family I have ever experienced. My host mother had a voice and equal rights and decision making that I never knew a woman could have. I realized then that the US was where I wanted to live.

After my year as an exchange student, I had to return to Georgia. I knew that once I went back to Georgia, I would not be allowed to apply for any US visa for at least two years due to the exchange program's requirement I had to follow. When it was time to go I cried the entire way to the airport, at the airport and on the plane. I could not imagine being back in the culture where my freedom was suppressed, and I was surrounded by a close-minded, conservative society.

I dreamed of coming back to the United States. That dream became more attainable when I was conducting a training at an American Library. During a lunch break, I came across this thick book that had a list of all colleges and universities in the US. I went through the entire book to find a list of colleges that offered full scholarships to international students. I identified 3 that I wanted to pursue. The only way I would have been able to attend college in the US was through a full scholarship.

That evening I researched all three of my options and only one college guaranteed all the expenses paid if you were accepted.

I eventually was able to apply to Berea College in Berea, KY, which offered full scholarships to international students.

I received an acceptance letter in 2008. I then realized that I had to start my life over in the US and that I would work hard to stay there. However, in August 2008, as I was planning my departure, Russia invaded Georgia, destroying my hometown, Gori, and forced me to leave my hometown. It had become very dangerous there because Russia was using bombs that had been banned by the international community and could explode at any moment. My family and I were able to escape from Gori and stay at our friends' apartment in Tbilisi. It's an unsettling feeling lying in bed wide awake and hearing a plane above you and wondering if that plane was about to drop a bomb on your house. I experienced a complex feeling of guilt and relief when leaving my family behind to come to the US. As I was getting ready to leave for the US, all flights out of Georgia were canceled by all airlines due to war except one. Georgian Airways were mandated by the Georgian Government to keep flights as scheduled and I was luckily on the only flight out of the country and into my new life in Berea, Kentucky. I remember sitting on that plane and wondering if it would make it out of the country or if it will be shut down by one of the Russian fighter jets as the invasion was still ongoing.

I am now a proud American. It took 10 years, thousands of dollars, and pages of paperwork, but I will never forget the day I was sworn in while raising my right hand. This is something that so many people across the world dream of and I was living it. I was able to achieve corporate career success, wealth, and freedom in the US that would have been unimaginable for a woman in Georgia.

Even with all of my success in the US, on January 31, 2022, my life came to an abrupt disruption. That morning, my Facebook Messenger app was blown up with messages from my Godmother. I learned that my 82-year-old grandfather had stabbed his own son 30 times while my uncle was asleep. I lost my composure when I saw the video of my grandfather, who looked frail and was led in handcuffs by the police. I felt grief and insufferable pity for my grandfather, who killed his own son in a drunken rage. My family is an example of generations of abusive parents who end up raising abusive children. I had to move across the world to escape this part of my life. My mother had lived in a role of a victim her entire life, and I had been raised to become her confidant, protector, and supporter from my abusive father.

When I left Georgia to move to the United States, my mother finally decided to divorce my father. He had become so enraged by her indifference and had thrown her against a mirror leaving her with a scar the length of her spine. That final act of violence was enough to drive her to finally leave the marriage. I was then expected to financially support my mother and my brother once I graduated from the MBA program. This is a common expectation of immigrants' families back home.

The horrific tragedy that transpired between my uncle and grandfather, was like a wakeup call for me. I realized that I had been working non-stop at a job I hated because I was expected to be the provider for two capable adults – my mother and my brother. Wealth acquisition was the primary motivation for me since I came to the United States as a student. However, dissatisfaction with the American dream has been growing within me for several years as I was desperately trying to quiet it through expensive vacations and fashion items. Through this unexpected death in my family, I realized how fleeting this life could be. I felt there was more to life than just working 12-hour days and living for a vacation. I wanted to find my purpose and find my authentic self. I hired a career coach to help me understand my feelings and through the coaching sessions I realized that no money could satisfy my desire for a purposeful life. Yet, I still didn't know what that meant for me. I just knew I had to find my authentic self and find my purpose in life at any cost. I decided it was time to take a year of sabbatical to find the answers I was seeking.

In 2021, I quit my corporate career and embarked on a year of sabbatical to find my true passion and purpose in life. This decision led me to travel to 12 countries, write three books, and start two new businesses within 12 months. In my personal life, I reconciled with my mother, surrounded myself with like-minded friends, and currently enjoy a fulfilling romantic relationship. Although financially, I took a set back by leaving my corporate career, I have elevated myself to higher levels in society, collaborating with people who are successful business owners, politicians, and impactful leaders.

Here is the story of how my two businesses were born. The idea of Christian Professionals of Atlanta was born when a friend and I discussed how difficult it is for professionals to meet other Christians in the same walk of life. A simple Google search for keywords such as Christian meetups or Christian professional organizations in Atlanta led to zero results. So, we decided why not start our own organization? And that is how Christian Professionals of Atlanta was born. It now successfully operates to bring business leaders within the Atlanta community to encourage them to become stronger servant leaders within the organization and within the community. We also organize service projects with various non-profit organizations within the city of Atlanta.

Our vision is to grow this organization to become Christian Professionals of America with a chapter in every major city in the United States. Our vision is to build an organization known for serving the community, building up people, and having a positive impact in our country. With a big vision that serves many people, an incredible thing happens. People want to become part of something bigger than themselves and join the movement that brings the positive change.

I started my coaching business Find Courage to Change while not pursuing another business idea as I was already busy building Christian Professionals of Atlanta. I had written a book called Finding Courage to Change, which talks about how to overcome childhood trauma and not let it define who you are as an adult. I wrote this memoir in two days while I was on a silent retreat at monastery as part of my sabbatical. I decided to give 50% of book sales to an organization called Saprea, which exists to liberate our society from child sexual abuse. As a thriving adult of childhood abuse, I am making efforts to educate people about her healing journey and spread a message of hope to people I encounter who also went through similar experiences.

As more people approached me, asking questions, seeking guidance, and sharing personal details about their lives, I knew I had to figure out a way to help them beyond just sharing my book with them. Thus, I pursued Personal Excellence Life coach certification and began my coaching business to help people become better versions of themselves. I help clients figure out what they truly want in life and how to get there by breaking limiting beliefs that are holding them back from living the life of their dreams.

By breaking down the conventional lifestyle, I was able to embrace my creativity, passions, and purpose, leading to a life beyond my expectations. I learned to live in the moment and not conform to societal expectations. I treat my past experiences as a sacred gift to be shared with others. My purpose in this book is to pass on the message that change is good for evolution, healing, and growth. I come from a developing country with a poor socio-economic background. My life outlook growing up was to be a wife and a stay-at-home mom, but I dreamed of a big life. Looking back at where I came from, sometimes it still amazes me what I was able to achieve, and I am in awe of all the experiences I have been blessed to have. I am enjoying the kind of freedom I never dreamed of having when growing up.

Ana Megrelishvili

Ana Megrelishvili is the founder of Christian Professionals of Atlanta, a networking organization focused on bringing Atlanta's leaders together to achieve a positive impact on the community through service.

Ana's passion for making a positive impact on the world has taken her on the path of working with non-profits when she became board member of Gift-Wrapping Stars for Children and gala committee chair for Saprea.

Ana helps adults find their own path to positive change in their lives through her coaching business, Find Courage to Change. As a thriving adult of childhood abuse, Ana is making efforts to educate people about her healing journey and spread a message of hope to people she encounters who also went through similar experiences. She documents her journey to healing in her book "Finding Courage to Change".

Ana holds a BS in business management from Berea College and an MBA from the University of Kentucky. She enjoys Latin dancing, volunteering, and creating new recipes in her free time.

Learn more at:

findcouragetochange.com

PowerfulFemaleImmigrants.com

AGAINST ALL ODDS

Dr Farah Sultan

I was rejected for a visa to the US once again, not for the first or second but the third time in two years, dashing all my hopes of ever fulfilling the great American dream.

I was born and raised in a small town, Ranchi, in India. I grew up in a very modest home, but my parents sacrificed all their earnings to give my brother, sister, and me a good education. I gained my early education at Loreto Convent in Ranchi, founded by the nuns of the Irish Branch of the Blessed Virgin Mary (IBVM). I received a great education and made the best of friends. I grew up with a vision of one day becoming a doctor to help alleviate suffering and pain in those with illness and disease.

I worked hard and became the first in my family to go to medical school. I earned a scholarship to attend one of the finest medical schools in India, Christian Medical College in Vellore.

My dream was to train as a doctor in America to be able to bring to fruition my vision of being of service to others. However, this dream was shattered when I was rejected for a visa to visit the United States after an interview at the US consulate in New Delhi.

Not to be deterred, I went to the UK and trained in medicine. I studied to pass the difficult exams to be awarded the MRCP (Membership of the Royal College of Physicians).

I was then able to reapply for and be granted the opportunity to go to the land of the brave and the free. With just a suitcase of my belongings, I stepped off the plane, ready to begin a new chapter of my life.

The road was not all smooth. I had many trials and tribulations, but with grit and determination, I was able to overcome disappointment, setbacks, and frustrations along the way until I faced the biggest challenge ever – the loss of my own health.

I found myself being wheeled to the operating room for an emergency cesarean section at Texas Women's Hospital in Houston, as my labor from hell began to unfold. My blood pressure, heart rate, and oxygen were dropping to dismal levels. My baby's heart rate was abnormally low, too. I thought we wouldn't make it. Fortunately, we both survived, with my baby ending up in the neonatal intensive care unit for several days with tubes and intravenous lines all over his tiny body.

We eventually made it home, only to find out that my body was failing me.

Despite my son's birth being the most momentous and joyous part of my life, I was experiencing post-partum blues, intense fatigue, pounding headaches, hair loss, brain fog, poor sleep, loss of libido, and abdominal pain, as though my insides were being scraped out.

Instead of losing the weight I had gained over pregnancy, I started blowing up and gaining more weight. My body was just not working right, and I couldn't understand why. Why had all my years of training in medical school and residency not prepared me to take care of my own health challenges? I sought help from my doctor, and she simply blew me off saying it was normal and part of being a new mom and stressed-out resident.

A woman knows her own body, and I knew something wasn't right. It was years later that I found out that I had Hashimoto's thyroiditis, which caused my immune system to attack my own thyroid gland, along with underlying food intolerances, which were wreaking havoc with my health and well-being.

It was only when I was able to get to the root cause of my illness by diving deep into testing, finding the right mentors to work with, and getting further educated in functional and integrative medicine that I was able to transform my health. This was such a life-changing event that I could no longer go back to practicing medicine in the conventional model that I had been taught in medical school. I was done prescribing drugs for my patients that acted as mere band-aids and were wrought with adverse side effects. At the end of the day, they did not resolve the issues; they merely covered up the symptoms.

It was a turning point in my career when I founded Vitalogy Wellness Center and started helping women transform their lives, one person at a time.

I have not looked back since February 2014, when I started helping women unveil the underlying causes of their concerns and turn things around using a holistic, lifestyle-based approach. Since then, my team and I have helped thousands of women get back their energy, sleep, mental clarity, sex drive, glowing hair and skin, and hormone balance. These women can lose body fat and maintain healthy lean muscle mass without starving and counting calories.

They can improve their moods and focus rather than feeling irritable and unstable.

How, you may ask, did they achieve these remarkable results? Here are the key pillars of the ***Mandala Method*** that can help transform lives:

- Nutrition: The diets should be personalized to the individual since we are all unique.
- Gut Health: The gut plays a pivotal role as the foundation for our immune system, as well as in facilitating our metabolism through the liver and the absorption of essential nutrients. Additionally, it has a significant impact on the balance of our microbiome.
- Hormone Balancing: This involves balancing hormones by measuring and using natural approaches or bioidentical hormones. The hormones include female hormones, adrenal (stress hormone), thyroid, insulin, and leptin (satiety hormone), to name a few.
- Mind-Body Balance: This is achieved by balancing the neurotransmitters that concern emotional health, motivation, memory, mood, and overall well-being and stress management.
- Fitness: Movement and exercise are part of living a healthy life.
- The central pillar of the Mandala, where everything interconnects, is the education piece, as we must learn the tools to help ourselves in the future as well.

This is a tried-and-tested method that has worked for many women. If you would like to learn more about the Mandala Method and are wondering if it would be a good fit for you, then click here and schedule a free 15-minute call. As a bonus, you'll get a free e-book on how to balance your hormones through nutrition.

CTA:

Book a free call with us and download a free digital copy of my e-book on nutrition for hormone health and balance.

https://nutrientdiets.aflip.in/vitalogyhormoneweightloss

Visit our website: https://vitalogywellnessandmedspa.com/

Follow us on Instagram: https://www.instagram.com/farahsultanmd/

TikTok: https://www.tiktok.com/@farahsultanmd?lang=en

Facebook: https://www.facebook.com/VitalogyWellness

Linked In: https://www.linkedin.com/in/farah-sultanmd-abfm-abaarm-38613ab3/

Listen to this story from Tracy Wright about her relief of fatigue, migraines, food addictions:

https://www.youtube.com/watch?v=whDExW67Lbk

Look out for my new book that's coming out soon to read in-depth about the Mandala Method!

Dr Farah Sultan

Dr Farah Sultan is a Medical Doctor, board-certified in Family Medicine and Functional and Regenerative Medicine. She has trained and worked in 3 continents: India, the UK, and the US. She is the Founder of Vitalogy Wellness and Med-Spa and the creator of the Mandala Method. She is an international award-winning speaker, author, and expert in sleep and hormone balance and has helped thousands of women regain their sleep, energy, and youthfulness without the use of addictive prescription medications. She lives with her husband and three children in Birmingham, Alabama, and loves to travel, read, garden, cook, and bio-hack her health and fitness.

PowerfulFemaleImmigrants.com

DREAMS: SEEDLINGS OF DIVINE GUIDANCE

Eda Walldorf, Venezuela

As we were together laughing, sharing stories, and breaking bread, a sudden and perhaps even "divine" thought planted itself in my mind. This was my chance, I thought, that perhaps I too could have a similar experience as my 19-year-old sister and perhaps our newfound friends could take me back with them to the United States. I could have one of my most deeply seeded dreams realized, I could finally learn English! There was one small issue, my bilingual sister was 19, but I was a mere 11 years old.

It was a cool summer night when my family and our American friends were all gathered around the grill in our beautiful backyard which hosted the likes of exotic birds such as toucans, colorful macaws, parakeets, and parrots. We had just met a lovely family who had come down to Venezuela for a month of exploration including visiting the tallest waterfall in the world located in the Amazon jungle: Angel Falls. In this unlikely gathering, the only way we could communicate was via the bilingual member of our group, my 19-year-old sister, who had just returned from a foreign exchange program in Ohio, where she had briefly met them and offered to host them in the capital city of Caracas, where we lived.

I was enthralled with this beautiful family, and the thought of traveling to the States with them consumed my heart. I then approached my mom and insisted that I travel back with them. Understandably, my sister did not want to translate this audacious request. There was also the objection that my mom presented to me, as she said, "Eda, when I leave you to spend the night at your cousin's house, you cry uncontrollably all night and I must drive 45 minutes there, and then back to pick you up in the middle of the night. I'd be unable to do that if you were a whole country's flight away." I had an especially close attachment to my mom at this young age, the thought of leaving her behind seemed devastating. Somehow, though, I convinced my mom and myself that I would be fine on my own, and still to my astonishment, she believed me. I argued that my 12-year-old sister could come with me, and we would keep each other company. But when we approached her about this idea, her answer was a resounding "No." Through some miracle my mom eventually gave into my suggestion, and my oldest sister agreed to translate the request. The first few of many seemingly large obstacles had been overcome. The American family was taken aback at first and as we started discussing all the requirements needed for me to be able to go to the States with them, it all seemed near unreal. Nevertheless, the conversation persisted.

All in all, the odds seemed beyond impossible. The obstacles kept adding up: we needed to book five plane tickets (the family was flying back home with numerous layovers, including a week's stopover in Disney World). We also quickly realized that my passport was expired, as was my U.S. Visitor's visa. Furthermore, I'd need parental permission from the U.S. Embassy to leave with a foreign family as a minor. I also needed my school's permission to miss a few months of course work, and finally I would also need the Ohio's school superintendent's approval to attend school in the U.S. while living with them (they could not very well leave me at home alone, while everyone went back to school and work upon their return).

We only had one business day to get this punch list of items completed, and they would be flying home the following morning. It was in these next moments where faith, and divine guidance prevailed, and revealed their true powerful nature. Much to everyone's surprise, we got every single one of the items on our list completed within the unreasonable time frame given. I had a renewed passport and visa in hand. I also had five confirmed plane tickets matching their exact plane itinerary and seating arrangement. I had the U.S. Embassy granted parental permission, as well as both schools' green light. It was beyond miraculous that all this came together. This instance of divine guidance allowed for a seamless flow, which was unparalleled to anything I've since experienced. Before we all could blink, I was packed, and on an airplane, dreaming about living in the United States with my newly adopted lovely American family.

Unfortunately, when reality came flooding in, tears were indeed shed the first night of arrival at their home in Cincinnati. However, these were the only tears that would shed until five months later, when my natural family came to Cincinnati to retrieve me, and I had to say goodbye to my new beautiful American parents, and this wonderful experience that had just realized my dreams.

When an experience like this shapes your early years, and alters the rest of your destiny, it reveals some rich and wonderful truths. Ultimately, this experience unveiled the profound mystery and latent reality of divine guidance in my life. There truly is an inner voice within each of us, which can shape our reality into as powerful an experience as we'll allow. I have a deep conviction that this power is readily available to each of us, and it's not confined to the few that have had the privilege of being open to exploring and experiencing it. It's a matter of quieting the chatter of our surroundings. It's about allowing that inner knowing, or that inner calling, to whisper into our lives to guide and inspire us. The gift of being able to heed this inner voice, which prompted me at such a young age to pursue my dreams (despite having all the odds against us), changed my perspective, as well as the course of many lives forever. Although there is so much more to share beyond this short story regarding where I've been and all that I've experienced and overcome, this unique experience has remained foundational to my understanding of life's mysteries.

A few decades later, after completing high school and college in the United States, I met my husband and together we dedicated ourselves to a life of service to underprivileged teens in the States, Venezuela, Costa Rica, and Guatemala for several years. We had many ups and downs, and many struggles, including living off our fundraising efforts and other people's generosity, who supported our vision and mission to love on these beautiful souls. We lived abroad and back in the States for several years, during which time, and after two high risk pregnancies, we were blessed with our two amazing sons.

Upon returning to the States and spending the last years of my mother-in-law's life with her, we essentially had to start over. Our financial life was challenging to say the least. Where most of our friends had nearly a half a decade of building their resumes and climbing the corporate ladder, we had to start from scratch leaning on governmental programs to help cover our family of four's basic needs. It was a humbling and difficult time. We had two kids in diapers, and my husband's job was a 100% commission-based sales position with his family's real estate firm. As our kids grew, I was finally free to take a job teaching. I truly enjoyed diving into my professional life, but being an all-in individual, I would spend countless hours preparing lessons and grading. I found that my time at home with the children was being compromised, and that my efforts did not match my paycheck.

As I was sitting in front of my computer one evening looking simultaneously over a pile of papers to grade, and bills to pay, I thought to myself: "This can't be all there is to life." I knew in my heart there was more, the same way that I knew that night of the barbeque at my home in Venezuela that I was being drawn out to a deeper experience. That's when a thought was again planted in my heart: I should pursue real estate investing. But how?

Thinking back on this moment, I was flooded by an equally loud but inner voice called fear. This crippling whisper, which negates all our hopes and dreams, continues to be a source of hindrance along the journey in most of our lives. I personally have been victimized by fear, and have adopted several coping mechanisms, which have become crutches and hindrances to my growth (particularly in times of challenge and heart ache). Paradoxically at other times, fear has motivated me to look for alternate paths, and has spurred me on to deeper growth, creativity, and greater opportunity.

One of the many things that I have learned, and that I continue to grow in understanding about fear, is that we must allow ourselves to feel its full force and not cower from it. When we face our fears head on, and we allow ourselves to consider the worst, we diminish its power over us and come ahead on the other end. Facing our fears allows for a deeper understanding with our intellectual and emotional minds. A previously numbing or even paralyzing fear can truly be overcome when we strip its perceived power over us. The moment we bow down to our fear in defeat, we in fact, give our power away. Once we realize that we do not have to hide from it, or feel powerless, we can walk through and past the fear. We can come out on the other end, feeling our ever-present inner strength. When we focus on what's possible and reclaim our own power, we can in fact have the courage and strength to keep moving forward. In this moment I felt the duality of what was possible, as well as that which felt impossible. Despite our many challenges, my desire for something greater persisted, and I became again attentive to that faint inner voice that reminded me that this was a calling to heed. I had an intuitive knowing that there was something within me that was special, even powerful, that kept me pursuing a richer life experience.

Thinking back on this new inner voice guiding me again towards something that seemed impossible, towards a life in real estate investing, when we did not have any funds to cover such a lofty enterprise, seemed almost absurd. But then again, just like all things that are meant to be, and that are brought forth via divine guidance, after many ups and downs, a deep conviction to pursue this opportunity, and many false starts and failed attempts, we finally began a life changing process in my professional life that would alter our financial lives forever.

It all started with one house flip, where we secured a very small percentage of the profits. From there, we went on to the next, and then to the next. I went from house flipping, to building a spec home, to then going back to school to get a second degree from the New York School of Interior Design. I got my general contractor's license in commercial and residential building and continued into real estate development. Since then, we've been able to amass a nice rental portfolio consisting of single, small multi-family and large multifamily apartments, which at this time, amounts to just over 2,500 units, in several states in the nation. The journey, although simplified and condensed in a few words, has come with many ups and downs, challenges, sacrifices, both heartbreaks and celebrations. There has been a great pursuit of knowledge, countless funds contributed towards the most renowned experts and securing the best education our money could buy. All this effort, risk, time, hard work, commitment, and action has led us to a very rewarding outcome towards financial independence and allowed us to build a multi-million-dollar enterprise.

We are now in the business of helping others achieve similar success: by sharing our wealth of knowledge and expertise in a way that helps our clients secure passive income, via investing in carefully curated real estate ventures. We invite our clients to leverage their time and money leaning on our combined decades of experience and knowledge, our continued due diligence, market studies, and our proven track record in real estate. My husband and I founded Walldorf Capital Ventures, which is one of many companies we manage within our real estate realm. Our ventures have been a foundational vehicle to growing our wealth. We have condensed all our accumulated experiential and educational learning of real estate investing into a fool proof offering to help our clients realize seamless, passive, and exponential growth for their economic well-being in pursuit of their own financial independence.

The realization of these dreams has been foundational in reassuring my certainty that all the dreams that continue to brew within me are still attainable and fully possible in my present and future reality. As I can look back and reminisce on the many experiences that have enriched my life, I realize that dreaming and listening to the inner voice has been instrumental in spurring me on towards continued growth and impact. As Malcom Forbes beautifully states, "When you cease to dream, you cease to live." This truth resonates deeply in my heart, as I've always felt like dreaming has been a lifeline in times of challenge and divine guidance in times of change and opportunity. There's an element of dreaming which acts as a guiding light towards their inception, but dreams without actions are void of fuel. As Walt Disney plainly expresses: "All our dreams can come true if we have the courage to pursue them." The dreams that have grown in my heart have translated into the seedlings that have spurred me on to flesh them out in my reality, with faith being a foundational ingredient, in pursuit of their realization. This faith, combined with tireless action, have been fueled by an obsession, commitment, and persistence to see them come into fruition; "For as the body without the spirit is dead, so faith without works [action] is dead also." (James 2:14-26).

I live in a constant dream world and my main challenge has been the trouble to sift through my many dreams and give the focus and attention to those that speak to my heart and align the most with my spirit. Once I have honed in on those "special" dreams, their resounding calling has spurred me on to pursue, plan, and organize my thoughts into actionable steps to see them come into fruition. The trouble with our hearts is that most of us either ignore this small inner voice, listen to its parallel cousin "fear," or simply label it all as an "impossibility" or as too far-fetched. Sometimes, we go as far as questioning our own deservedness of these dreams and their perceived impossibility. We think too little of ourselves, too little of the divine guidance available to each of us, and too little of what's possible. We lack both a child-like imagination, as well as a child-like faith. I've experienced these same crippling thoughts, and continually fall victim to forgetting all that is possible and the truth of our powerful nature. It is a moment-by-moment journey, in which I constantly remind myself every single day that I am deserving of a life full of love, abundance, and adventure.

It has been my heart's desire to pass this sense of wonder, possibility, and adventure to my own children, and make it an integral part of our life experience. They have both taken this desire on, by leaving home, learning new languages, and being curious and open to experiencing new cultures. Already at a young age, they are both tri-lingual; my oldest having already lived in Taiwan for a year as an exchange student, at the young age of 17. In the next few days, both my sons will be headed on their own independent adventures overseas for a year to Brazil and to New Zealand. My youngest is slated to become quadrilingual by the end of next year and hopes to pursue a career in engineering upon his return.

I feel blessed beyond measure and cannot help but keep reminiscing on all the sacred moments in my life where divine guidance has given me the opportunity and clarity to be still and listen. I feel infinitely grateful for the life I've come to experience. In my gratitude, I am persuaded to believe that I am worthy, that I have infinite intelligence as well as God's guidance always on my side. I truly believe that I'm fully equipped to pursue my dreams and burst through as many "impossibilities" as life places in front of me for the remainder of my life in my pursuit of adventure and service.

Eda Walldorf

Eda Walldorf was born in Caracas, Venezuela. At the young age of 11, she traveled to the United States to learn English, and later moved with her family to Cincinnati, OH where she attended high school, at age 14. She graduated from Denison University, as well as Hollins University, Paris, France campus. Later in life, she pursued another degree at the New York School of Interior Design. While at Denison, she met her husband of 24 years, Nathan, with whom she not only shares two beautiful sons, Thatcher and Andrew-Lewis but also a career and passion for all-things real estate.

She has dedicated her professional life to investing in real estate, as well as managing their portfolio of real estate holdings. She is a linguist, an interior designer by training, a commercial and residential general contractor, multifamily apartment investor, and developer. She has nearly two decades of experience in real estate and brings her knowledge, growth-mindset, and expertise to serve their clients in carefully curated passive investing opportunities. They currently manage a portfolio of nearly 900 units across several states, and are invested in over 2,500 units passively & actively. Eda continues to pursue her passion for innovation and growth in the field of sustainable development.

Eda believes in pursuing a life path shaped by her dreams, via divine guidance, fueled by passion and an unwavering commitment to action. She and her husband are passionate about their service to others and have dedicated many years of their lives to serving underprivileged teens in countries such as Venezuela, Costa Rica, the United States, and Guatemala.

They currently live in Chattanooga, TN and Anna Maria Island, FL.

PowerfulFemaleImmigrants.com

GENIUS IS THE SPIRIT
360-DEGREE VIEW AND LIVING IN FREEDOM

Paulina Amador, Mexico

I am a filmmaker and a rebel. I learned to think outside of the box, being a Genius became my heart's deepest desire.

From an early age, I reacted against the traditional status quo of my upbringing in Guadalajara, Mexico. Often feeling as if I were in a mental straight jacket, at first, like many children, I was combative with teachers when I sought answers for the many contradictions in what was being taught. At age 13, my curiosity led me to delve into a wide variety of books and other ways of thinking that were outside of the scope of traditional education.

I loved nature and spent a lot of time exploring it. I gravitated towards other people who were also attempting to free themselves from the more traditional ways. My active imagination led me to question everything.

I quickly realized our culture can be narrow-minded wherein women are often treated as if their importance has nothing to do with their minds. This led to my desire to escape and to travel the world. I first moved to Canada at age 18 with my best friends, Anedh and Isabel. We were able to survive for a few months, as I had some savings from my job - being a simultaneous translator at EXPO Guadalajara, México. The international hub for the nexus between business, sustainability, and culture, it hosts the largest international book fair in the Americas, better known as the FIL, attracting worldwide Nobel Laureates, including Gabriel García Marquez. My friends and I attended this event year after year. And now, this very book you are reading, will be presented at this year's 2023 fair.

While living in the city of Vancouver, I found a sense of freedom in that more open-minded country, but we quickly ran out of money. My sense of adventure didn't let me down and we hitchhiked to the countryside town of Keremeos, where we worked harvesting apples and peaches. Imagine that! We had all grown up in private schools in Mexico, and we certainly didn't fit within the mold of our society. Surrounded mostly by male farmers, we were the center of attention and felt worried about our safety. Tired of climbing huge ladders, up and down all day, we decided to travel back to Mexico by train. In those times and perhaps still today, it was guaranteed to have a chicken as your passenger neighbor, and locals cooking fresh tacos inside the train with the dirtiest water there is. We were happier than ever, as we felt accomplished in our initial quest for FREEDOM.

Soon after my return, I received the most shocking experience one can have. I found myself floating on the ceiling of a room at the Mexico Americano hospital, looking down at my body on a surgical metal table with my belly cut wide open. Perhaps, due to the effects of the anesthesia, I was aware of being outside of my body with a 360-degree view, in a state of weightlessness. I could hear melodic voices from afar, as well as seeing many beautiful colorful beings floating like spirits radiating soft pastel tones; they formed a circle surrounding my body from above. I knew these beings were helping me come back from what seemed a faraway place, yet so close. Suddenly, the most beautiful melody started to play, I began to sing this heavenly tune, leading me back to my body. Quickly afterwards, there I was waking up to a new life free from more than a kilo of tumors that had been removed from my abdomen. The diagnosis was unknown, as the doctors couldn't find the source of these formations, nor could they tell me if they would form again. My recovery was questionable. My future was at stake!

I walked into the unknown with a feeling of uncertainty. What had happened to me, and why? **The one thing I was sure of was I had been given a second opportunity to live. I had seen and experienced the grace of God, the world of spirit, and I was determined to discover more about the mystery of this unseen power I had encountered.**

My life's purpose completely shifted. Soon after I recovered, I zeroed my mind in on a spiritual journey. I was driven to understand the answers to some of life's biggest questions: Where do we come from, and where are we going? What is consciousness? Is immortality real?

I moved to New Mexico to attend a spiritual school, where I learned all about the Native American ways. Initiated into their sacred ceremonies and the mind-bending disciplines of board breaking and walking on fire, I became a Kundalini yoga teacher and a certified Cranial Sacral therapist. These practices needed to be engaged in a trance state, so **I learned to allow the invisible power within me do the work; all these experiences led to my healing and furthered my**

understanding that we are more than our physical body. While living near Santa Fe, I also earned an associate arts degree in multimedia. I had already studied Graphic Design and Photography at ITESO, Universidad de Guadalajara where I began to develop my unique voice and style. Often breaking the rules of composition, my artistic photography work challenges the boundaries of linear perspectives of reality, and I often focus in seeing life through the lens of the soul and the world of the unseen. I was hired by renowned photographer in Santa Fe, Cathy Maier Callanan, and her husband, Reid Callanan, owner of the international Santa Fe workshops. I debuted my first photography and multimedia exposition. Throughout the years I have been a passionate photographer, and now I am an official contributor to the world-renowned Getty Images agency.

I met various interesting figures, including the celebrated Mexican television host and producer Raúl Velasco, and Charles Collins, the grandson of Dorothy Stimson Bullitt, broadcaster, realtor, and philanthropist who founded King Broadcasting Company (KING 5 – TV Channel) in Seattle. Charles and I became great friends, almost like a father/daughter relationship. We seemed to have known each other from another time, and he fulfilled my absent father place and became my patron throughout my stay in New Mexico.

At the beginning of the year 2000, I moved back to Mexico. I always loved the ocean, so this time I went to Puerto Vallarta. I taught yoga at the nearby Four-Season Hotel in Punta Mita, Nayarit, and soon afterwards met Lynne Bairstow, head of marketing for the world-class luxury resort which features two Jack Nicklaus Signature Golf Courses and some of the world's most coveted high-end residential real estate. She was another angel on my path, teaching me all about the corporate world. As her assistant, we worked with the top publications, Condé Nast Traveler, Rob Report, Forbes, and many others. But wait, she also loved yoga herself and was a very spiritual, kind, and successful businesswoman, I felt at home. In the coming years, I founded my multimedia company, Holo-graphics Re-defining Media, which was eventually hired by the same outstanding team in Punta Mita and many other international clients.

Having become a successful graphic designer, I moved to Barcelona, Spain to study filmmaking at the CECC of Catalunya. While there, I had the opportunity to witness the timeless and majestic basilica, "Sagrada Família," the creation of my favorite genius architect, Antonio Gaudí. His work broke all established rules, his style is characterized by freedom of form and organic unity. While finishing my studies in Spain, **I felt a deep inner call to continue my spiritual path. No one had yet answered the question of my lifetime: Is immortality real? I thought to myself, the Alchemists who pursued the elixir of life that grants eternal youth and cures all diseases are the Geniuses of our time. They are always ahead of the status quo, their creations lead the way forward, giving birth to new paradigms in times to come. I followed my passion, deciding to open my mind to new doors of possibility and determined to make my own path. I researched the greatest minds in history, and the results were shocking - all were distinguished Genius men.** Amongst them were Nikola Tesla, Albert Einstein, Isaac Newton, Leonardo da Vinci, and Socrates. It was undeniable: the one thing present in my search results – or shall we say absent – was the recognition of women. **I asked myself, how can humankind, or in this case 'mankind' manage to write 'his-story' to exclude the genius minds of women and their** extraordinary accomplishments? Is anyone to blame, or are we all complicit in this most epic conspiracy?

I embarked on a journey of discovery; my soul was set on fire! I decided to produce and direct my groundbreaking documentary, *EVOLUTION: The Genius Equation.* I interviewed some of the greatest thinkers and scientists of our time and began to see life from a whole new perspective. I learned that because history was mostly written by men, many Genius women were not acknowledged. I have always been puzzled as to why there is so much inequality and injustice everywhere I look. I found myself in the midst of a struggle, unable to solve what seemed like an endless fight for human rights. Then a greater understanding struck at the heart of my life's dilemma. **While participating at an event at *Ramtha's School of Enlightenment*, I heard JZ Knight brilliantly speaking about her life experience as a patent creator and how, *"the fundamentals of Genius are a passion for the future and ambition for understanding."* She continued, *"Everyone has sort of staked out a territory of passion and ambition. And it is truly based upon working for the rights of human beings. That is a noble enterprise. But enlightenment is so bizarre in that you don't fight for women's rights; you teach women how to be a genius. The one right that we all have is to be divine. That divine right leads us to genius."***

Ultimately, I asked myself, if having a divine right sets us on equal ground, can we dispel the illusion of separation based on race, gender, and class? Then, perhaps, we could alleviate human suffering. During this event and many more that came afterwards, I learned about quantum physics, the power of the mind, how to focus and manifest the reality I desire, and how to heal myself. There is a famous saying in neuroscience: *"What fires together wires together."* In other words, whatever you focus on, is.

It seems to me, that the way forward is to write the story of how we all become Geniuses. In 2016, during its creation, I found out that Linda Evans the acclaimed actress of Dynasty was my neighbor, I presented her the script. She was thrilled to learn about my project and in her own words, said: *"This is a manual on the mind. I don't want anyone else to narrate it but me."* I couldn't have found a more beautiful voice to represent the essence of my film.

I founded WEGeniusMinds Productions, a full-service, multimedia international production company committed to unfolding the genius within us all. **My visual masterpiece, *EVOLUTION: The Genius Equation* is now streaming on Amazon, Apple TV and YouTube movies. It inspires us to think for ourselves and to explore our unlimited potential**, therefore creating a new paradigm for our understanding of Genius. I think it's important that people have the freedom to dig deeper and follow their curiosity. Many feel they are not allowed to think for themselves. It is the biggest problem in our current society that people don't value their own thoughts. **Physicist Michio Kaku says, 'All kids are born geniuses, but are crushed by society.' My dear friend from my days in Santa Fe, Charles Collins, is the executive producer. He has now been my best friend, investor, and supporter for over twenty years. After having all the visas, a foreigner can possibly have; family, tourist, work, green card, I am now a free citizen of the United States of America.** I have made my home in Washington State.

When we follow our true nature, our intuition, our knowingness, equality finds us and in giving back through our art whichever craft it may be, we find a whole new sense of value and honor for all. The universe provides to us in unlimited ways. I found that the journey to Genius is closest to my heart, as it's always about new discoveries and downloading the future! And here is the best part, according to Michio Kaku, *"96% of our universe hasn't been discovered yet."* **Never waste a second opportunity. It may be your million-billion-dollar-biggest deal, a new business venture, or a whole new life that's calling you from afar to be better, brighter, and more evolved, your genius equation.**

Make your life your own, no one else knows better than you. The wisdom gained from your choices is your pearl, your strength, your evolution.

Remember, there will always be someone ahead or behind you, comparing yourself with others is futile.

If you follow the voice of your spirit, it will always lead the way forward.

Paulina Amador

Artist – Storyteller – Documentarian – Transcendentalist – Explorer – Futurist – Alchemist

Creator, Director, and Producer of the groundbreaking feature documentary, EVOLUTION: The Genius Equation, Paulina Amador is the founder of Holo-graphics Re-defining Media and WEGeniusMinds Productions. Passionate and inquisitive, she refuses to shy away from asking big questions, inspiring curiosity and wonder in her viewers. Her extensive work as a Fine Art Photographer informs her cinematic style – producing films that are visually sumptuous and mindfully evocative. Paulina studied Documentary Filmmaking at the New York Film Academy and at the CECC in Barcelona, Spain; Graphic Design and Photography at ITESO University in Guadalajara, México. She is a member and contributor to the world-renowned Getty Images agency, as well as the international fine art photography organization and online magazine, Lens Culture. Owner of CF Domain, Investors, LLC a Real Estate Investment Company. Born in Guadalajara, Mexico, Paulina currently resides in the Pacific Northwest.

Honored to be a Selected Speaker at the Premiere Seattle TEDx Shorts event on August 16, 2023, TEDx had this to say about Paulina: "Blending her gifts as a Visionary Storyteller with her journey a Spiritual Explorer, she elevates the art of storytelling to the magic of a Documentary Alchemist. Driven by a purpose to create impact, she crafts narratives that not only captivate audiences but also inspires them to transcend ordinary realms by igniting their own unique genius."

She has interviewed best-selling authors and futurists, Dr. Michio Kaku (City University of New York), David Gelernter (Yale University), Dr. Chiara Marletto (Oxford University), Dr. Norman Doidge (author, *The Brain that Changes Itself*), Dr. Feryal Ozel (University of Arizona, Event Horizon Project), Jason Padgett (author, *Struck by Genius*), Paris Reid (artist), Philippa Gregory (author, *The Other Boleyn Girl, The White Queen*), Dr. Poppy Crum (Dolby Laboratories, Stanford University), Margaret Starbird (author, *The Woman with the Alabaster Jar*), JZ Knight (author, *State of Mind*, inventor, patented Blu Room technology), Ramtha (Spiritual Teacher of Ramtha's School of Enlightenment), Dr. Stanley Krippner (Saybrook University), Dr. Sam Sternberg (Columbia University).

Paulina is now working on her own book, the handbook of *EVOLUTION: The Genius Equation, A Roadmap to Genius*. She is creating a mini-series sequel to her feature film documentary and is also producing and directing a new documentary, *BIONIC Transcendental Realities*. Selected by Marquis Who's Who for their illustrious 2024 edition, her work as a renowned Director and Producer of visionary films and multi-media projects continues to reach audiences worldwide.

Watch EVOLUTION: The Genius Equation @ https://linktr.ee/wegeniusminds

Subscribe to her newsletter at:

wegeniusminds.com

PowerfulFemaleImmigrants.com

CATALYSTS OF CHANGE: THE CORE FAMILY OFFICE STORY

Puja Sohi and Avneet Kaur, India

We are so grateful for this chapter and this opportunity. We have built the Core Family Office with courage and passion for transparency. This book is our first attempt to showcase our company as immigrant women. It has absolutely been a pleasure to think about our lives again and learn about what brought us here, why are we built this way. It's also a great review to lap the last 6 years and think about the next 6 years.

In this chapter, we hope that you would learn more about Puja and I. She is making me write the chapter and probably won't even read it till it's a bestseller. We have the most interesting relationship ever. We have been called many things, but we are none of them. When we met, we were never friends, absolutely not related and almost had nothing in common. We see things completely differently and can't help but collaborate. Since the day we met, we have had this energy we generated together, somehow I don't think I can do it without her, and she says the same to me. It's a relationship you must have with your co-founder. She is my Co-founder. We met, and I asked her 2000 plus questions. We laughed on the most nonsense topics and I told her my dreams and this company I have been dreaming about, she said it had never been done before and could be done! I was honestly not sure how she would handle my straightforward personality, I thought she would say that's great, I hope you can do it. Instead she said 'let's do it' I told her, I don't know how long it would take to build it or bring home revenue, but I know technically it can be done. She said 'we can figure out the rest!' Core was born over a Steak Lunch in 2017.

It was a huge move for two immigrant women with no institutional backing to decide to step into the family office space, a 6 trillion dollar industry according to CNBC as of 2021 and increasing fast. Core has made the model available for 5m to 100m dollar families/individuals without the hefty fees or AUM requirements. This is a huge disruption in Wealth Management, Real Estate, Lending, Insurance, Succession and Tax. We decided we didn't just want a transaction, we wanted to earn relationships, we wanted to build families with education, stability with succession and most of all legacy with Family Office.

I will do my best to not make this a monologue. I have had a very interesting life.

My journey began in India, where I was born into a military family. From the very beginning, my life was marked by constant relocations. I think I have lived in 13 different states during the first 17 years of my life. Each move brought new challenges and opportunities, from adapting to distinct cultures within India, learning to make new friends and finding my place in the world. It wasn't always easy, but these experiences taught me the value of embracing change with an unwavering spirit and learning from every new chapter in life.

Despite the challenges, my family's support and love served as an anchor, grounding me during times of upheaval in India in the 80's and 90s. As a military family a sense of loyalty and a sense of service is in our DNA. We are 3rd generation Military since Indian partition in 1947.

When I turned 17 in 1997, life presented me with another thrilling adventure—a pivotal moment that would change the course of my destiny. My dad made the daring decision to leave our homeland and pursue the American Dream. Ofcourse, came with it an amazing opportunity of education in the vibrant city of Los Angeles. The journey to a foreign land, far from the familiar comforts of home, was both exhilarating and terrifying. I knew nothing at 17, as a Junior in High School in El Camino Real in Woodland hills, Ca. While my counterparts were taking SATs, I had no idea I even needed to attempt them! I still don't remember if I ever took the SATs! I took 6 months off after 12th grade to research my next steps. Los Angeles Pierce College had a wonderful program to transfer to UCLA which worked wonders for me. I worked hard and transferred as a valedictorian to the prestigious UCLA. I majored in Middle East Politics, driven by my insatiable curiosity about the human condition and the complexities of politics in the region. India was in a political turmoil and seeing riots first hand made me question human psychology. I found my place in various extracurricular activities, like joining the Bhangra team and even running for the position of UCLA President. After completing my studies at UCLA, I was drawn to the world of Wall Street, fueled by a desire to understand the mechanisms that influenced global economies. Working in the financial hub of the world was both exhilarating and demanding. The fast-paced environment demanded quick thinking and the ability to adapt to rapidly changing market conditions. After the 2008 collapse of Lehman Brothers, a significant player on Wall Street, something in me changed. The broken trust in Wall Street was an experience of a lifetime and served as a stark reminder of the interconnectivity of the global economy and the importance of understanding the intricacies of financial systems.

It was during these turbulent times that I began to appreciate the role of financial services in people's lives and the power it held in shaping their future and relocated to Los Angeles in 2009 married, settled and focused on our Family real estate brokerages started by my father in 2002.

Life has a way of bringing kindred spirits together, and in 2017, fate orchestrated a serendipitous encounter that united Puja and me. Despite our seemingly different paths, we discovered a shared vision—to redefine the world of financial services.

Puja has been through the same loss in 2008 in the financial industry that I felt but from the Retail banking world. When I met her at an insurance office, we started joking about being immigrant women running our business. Both of us recognized that we loved being independent and enjoyed transparency in financial products because of 2008. Puja was in real estate and Insurance when we met, and I was working with my dad in his commercial real estate brokerage, which is still our home broker on record!

Puja had piqued my interest because she saw what others didn't. I think she felt the same about me that's why I am writing this chapter 6 years after we met. Puja's journey has been one defined by resilience and compassion, shaped by her experiences growing up in the warm embrace of San Fernando Valley. Raised by a single mother, she learned from an early age the importance of love, support, and nurturing relationships. But life's trials did not spare her, and like all of us, she experienced her share of pain and heartache. However, these challenges only served to strengthen her heart of gold, making her a beacon of care and compassion for everyone she encountered.

Puja's career path led her to work at Bank of America and Washington Mutual, where she faced her own set of hurdles. The financial crisis of 2008 brought an influx of loan modifications, testing her capabilities and resilience as she navigated through uncertain times. In those moments of crisis, Puja displayed unwavering strength, guiding her team with grace and determination. Her leadership was a source of inspiration, as she tackled the complexities of the financial landscape with a deep love for helping others and creating meaningful connections.

Puja can get the tough work done. She is like water, she can mold herself and deal with any situation she has been given. She worked at Bank of America and helped in training a team with barely any help or knowledge herself, she also realized she lost trust in the system. This was an awakening for her too. It was 2008 that woke us both up and made us realize, there isn't a big brother looking out for you, rather, if you don't watch out, you could lose everything you earned and as an immigrant all our eggs were in one basket.

Why was this she thought and quickly licensed in Insurance to get herself and her family life insurance. She understood, this was guaranteed versus the market and she didn't want to lose all her life savings in her retirement years. She knew she had to watch out for her family and wanted to build her own company.

Beyond her professional life, Puja's heart was equally open to her personal experiences. Her family held a special place in her heart, and she cherished the memories of growing up with her beloved grandmother, Nani. Their bond was unbreakable, and the values of love, compassion, and determination instilled in her during those formative years were deeply rooted in her family's nurturing environment. She wanted to leave a legacy for her son and thought about all the ways how. When she was building Core, she spoke about how important it is for kids to learn young and help parents in the business just like the original family offices did like the Medici family from 1000 years ago.

Her journey in finance took her on a path of understanding the power of financial services in shaping lives. Witnessing the transformative impact that smart financial decisions could have on individuals and families ignited a spark within her. She recognized the potential for change and the opportunity to make a difference in the lives of those she served.

When fate brought Puja and me together in 2017, it was evident that our paths were destined to converge. Our friendship blossomed, and as we faced the triumphs and tribulations of building our business together, our bond only grew stronger.

Puja's role in Core Family Office went beyond her expertise in Insurance. She became a guiding light for our clients, a source of comfort and assurance during times of uncertainty. Her heart of gold extended to our team, fostering a nurturing environment where everyone felt valued and supported.

Her impact on the lives of our clients went beyond financial matters; it was a journey of empowerment, instilling confidence and hope in those we served. Puja's heart of gold became the heart of Core Family Office, guiding our decisions and shaping our approach. She also runs our Philanthropy initiatives at Core.

As we look to the future, Puja's legacy of compassion and determination lives on through the Core Family Office. Her story is one of resilience, love, and a commitment to making a positive impact on the lives of others. Puja's journey is a testament to the power of empathy and the profound change that can occur when we lead with our hearts.

In the chapters to come, the story of Puja, Core Family Office, and our shared vision of empowerment will continue to unfold. Together, we will continue writing this story of empowerment and transformation.

A Future of Empowerment and Transformation

As Avneet and Puja look to the future, they see a world where the Core Family Office continues to thrive. Their story is an inspiration to others, encouraging them to embrace their unique paths, overcome challenges, and forge unbreakable bonds in the pursuit of their dreams. Through Core Family Office, Avneet and Puja are creating a lasting legacy, one that will continue to empower generations to come.

In the end, it is not just the financial success that defines their story but the transformative power of friendship, compassion, and unwavering determination. Theirs is a story of empowerment and transformation—an ode to the human spirit's capacity to rise above and create a world where everyone has the opportunity to achieve financial freedom and build legacies that endure. This is the legacy of Core Family Office, and Avneet and Puja are excited to continue writing this story with each passing day.

Puja Sohi & Avneet Kaur

Puja Sohi, an adept professional at Core Family Office, specializes in insurance advisory services, tax planning, real estate management and relationship management. Her unwavering dedication lies in helping high net worth individuals and families actualize their financial goals through tailored and comprehensive solutions.

On the other hand, Avneet Kaur, also a seasoned expert at Core Family Office, focuses on risk management, wealth advisory services, and real estate management. She is dedicated to delivering personalized strategies that safeguard clients' assets and propel them towards their financial objectives.

Together, Puja and Avneet are integral members of the Core Family Office team, offering a wealth of combined expertise in wealth management, tax planning, risk assessment, and real estate management. Collaboratively, they provide holistic solutions that are meticulously aligned with each client's unique financial circumstances and aspirations.

The synergy between Puja's profound grasp of insurance advisory and tax planning intricacies and Avneet's proficiency in risk mitigation and wealth advisory creates a dynamic partnership. This dynamic duo exemplifies Core Family Office's steadfast commitment to empowering individuals and families, guiding them towards confident and secure financial futures.

Through their expertise and unwavering dedication, Puja and Avneet embody the Core Family Office ethos, setting a standard of excellence in personalized financial services. Their collaborative approach, refined over years of experience, ensures clients receive the highest level of attention and expertise, enabling them to make informed financial decisions and secure their financial futures with confidence.

CoreFamilyOffie.com
PowerfulFemaleImmigrants.com

BREAKING BROKE

Liza Quinones, Puerto Rico

I grew up as a mere statistic destined to repeat the same old story. Yet beneath the weight of those labels, I sensed a spark within me yearning to break free and paint my own destiny. I come from a single-parent household. I am a proud Puerto Rican, uprooted from the vibrant Isla to the cold embrace of the United States. As children, we don't pay attention to the trials and tribulations of our parents. Parents are supposed to shield their children from the harsh realities that life throws at us. But reality was unrelenting, shoving down disappointment and frustration until we were throwing up desperation and poverty.

My idyllic childhood came to a crashing end when, without warning, we were swept away to an unknown land. For me, it was abrupt and harsh. One moment, I was at my elementary school graduation, and the next, on a plane headed to who knows where. At the time, I was living with my paternal grandmother, and my parents had been divorced for over five years. My parents were chasing the American dream. All I knew at the time was that I did not ask to leave my beautiful island. I distinctly remember my mother giving us a different set of clothing: a wool sweater, long pants, and sneakers that were two sizes too big. We left like thieves in the night. I didn't even pack any of my toys or dolls, just the clothes on my back. I was scared, hungry, angry, and confused. I had not seen my mother in years and had no idea that day would create a barrier in our family. I did not know it then, but I would not see my grandmother for another decade, and my sense of security would disappear until I turned 30.

The ten-hour flight from San Juan, Puerto Rico, to Maine felt never-ending. As the plane's door opened and the blast of cold air rushed in, I shivered in my sweater. There was heavy snow falling, and it was colder than anything I had ever experienced in my short life. My body and mind could not comprehend how to function. I decided at that moment I would find some way to get back to my beautiful island.

Immediately, I despised the United States. I hated the cold, I hated the snow, and I hated the language that everyone spoke, but I could not understand. I was lost, confused, and overwhelmed in my new environment. Within a few days of us being in Maine, my mother, who was living with her sister at the time, was assigned to a women's shelter. Once settled in our eight-by-ten room, Mami went and registered us for school. She told my sister and me that on the first day, she would drop us off, but we had to take the bus home. The next morning, I found myself as the only child in English as a second language class who spoke Spanish. Everyone else spoke either Russian, French, or Albanian. We lived there for two years. I later found out that my family was the only one of color in the neighborhood and in my school.

Not being able to communicate with anyone was frustrating and extremely difficult. I had no friends or family. Getting to the bus was another mission. As luck would have it, the buses were color-coded, allowing me to navigate the system. As the bus bumped along the unfamiliar path home, I looked out the window, contemplating all the radical changes in my life. A group of children began whispering unintelligible things that I could not understand. As the whispers grew louder, I noticed that I was the target of their amusement. When I got up from my seat, I was called a monkey and other racial slurs. It took months to understand the daily oppressive stigma that suffocated the entire bus. I was pushed, yelled at, and bullied for months until one day, I punched the boy in the nose, broke it, and got kicked off the bus. No one saw my pain. I was told to suck it up and not react with violence. The harshness of the bullying chipped away at my self-esteem, but I found solace in my education. It would save me one day.

Years later, my mother relocated us to New York, and I moved in with my father. I had many difficulties in my teenage years and often let my anger get the best of me. I was broken in spirit and thought that nothing would get better. At some points, I wanted to accept my fate of being a statistic and living in poverty. It seemed like the easy way out. However, I graduated at the top of my class and got accepted to UMass Boston with a full scholarship. Living with my father was worse than dealing with racism and bullies; it was a relief to leave.

However, I became a statistic again when I learned I was 17 and pregnant. What was I going to do? Who could I turn to? How was I going to provide for another person when I couldn't provide for myself? I had left my father's house and moved in with my best friend. We rented a room from her aunt, who was on numerous drugs and delusional. I had a part-time job at a grocery store that paid $6 per hour. To be honest, I had no idea how we ate sometimes.

There I was, contemplating having a child by myself despite not even being able to eat three meals a day. Nonetheless, I had my baby and quit school. It was the birth of my son, Orion, that ignited that fire within me – a determination to provide him with a better future. My life began when I became a mother. I did not want him to live the life I had endured. He needed to know that there was more to life and that he could achieve greatness. However, that greatness had to start with me.

Many things changed once I made the decision to live a better life. It did not happen immediately, but I now had a plan. Forgiveness became the first stepping stone toward redemption. Reconnecting with my mother, I came to understand the complexities behind her decision to move to the United States. I pursued my education once again, this time earning a full scholarship to the University of Florida, which had family housing. I made the cross-country move to a city where I had no family and no friends. This time, I faced the unknown with courage. I finished school, got a great job, and even bought a car.

Just as life seemed on an upward trajectory, the housing market changed the landscape of America, sending my world into a spiral. I lost my job; I was facing eviction and had no clue where our next meal would come from. I felt hunger and desperation again. The failure nearly broke me, but I couldn't give up because it was no longer just about me. I learned some valuable lessons, but I found that I could be broken further and still come out thriving.

The housing market crash led me down a different path that ended with me on house arrest a few years later. I had worked for a man who hired me with the understanding I would look the other way in certain aspects of his business. He solved my problems the same day I got the eviction notice on my door. By this time, I had not only my son but a beautiful little girl to think about. I feared what would happen to my kids if I could not figure it out. I did not ask any questions when the man gave me a house to live in and a brand-new car to drive as a sign-on bonus. I should have known it was too good to be true, but I wasn't thinking. My first thought was survival. He gave me the one thing everyone in my family coveted – homeownership. I had the deed to my house; it was mine. I would never have to worry about evictions ever again. Little did I know that I would lose all of that, too.

I have learned that you must work hard for everything in this life. Nothing is ever given without a price, and you must decide whether you're willing to pay it. However, if you work hard for something, earn it, and duplicate it, no one can take it away from you because you can do it all over again. Looking back, I learned from him how to make money, how to build a business, and what not to do in business. Those are skills no one can take away from me.

As I look back on my life's tapestry, I see vibrant threads of resilience, courage, and love woven together. In 2010, I borrowed $5,000 and turned it into a multi-million-dollar business. My business was born out of desperation and sacrifice and became my beacon of hope. The challenges that once threatened to define me paved my path to greatness. For me, failure was not an option. I am the artist of my destiny; I know that within me lies the power to rise above any statistic, to be an inspiration, to break the cycle of brokenness, and to create a legacy. My legacy is helping others achieve their success as well. I am no longer the broken little girl from Puerto Rico with only desperation and hunger to keep her warm. I am a powerful immigrant woman.

Liza M. Quinones

Liza M. Quinones is a visionary entrepreneur and CEO, distinguished as the founder of two successful ventures, Quick Tax and Credit Solutions and Tax Ninja Pro LLC. With a steadfast commitment to financial literacy and empowering small business owners, Liza has established herself as a prominent figure in the tax and financial industry.

As the head of Quick Tax and Credit Solutions, Liza leads a dynamic financial solutions firm dedicated to increasing financial literacy and helping families achieve their financial goals. Through a range of services, including taxes, business solutions, credit repair, and business credit, her firm equips individuals and businesses with the tools to make educated, empowered financial decisions.

Additionally, Liza is the driving force behind Tax Ninja Pro LLC, a software company specializing in assisting tax professionals start, grow, and scale their tax businesses. Providing professional tax software, business coaching, sales training, marketing mastery, advance tax classes, and hands-on tax preparer support, Tax Ninja Pro has helped over 100 tax professionals achieve six- and seven-figure incomes.

With a bachelor's degree in accounting and an impressive 15-year tenure as a tax strategist, Liza possesses a wealth of expertise in the tax industry. Furthermore, she has excelled as a business coach, achieving certification as a 10X Business Coach and earning recognition as one of Grant Cardone's esteemed Elite Business Coaches. A charismatic speaker and author, Liza shares her knowledge and insights to inspire others to achieve their entrepreneurial dreams.

Liza's entrepreneurial acumen and determination have borne remarkable fruit. Within just five years of founding her tax firm, she successfully transformed it into a multi-million-dollar enterprise, setting a precedent for excellence.

Driven by a powerful vision, Liza and her teams aim to impact the lives of one million families by empowering them to make educated, informed financial decisions that lead to abundant lives.

With main offices located in Tampa, Florida, and Dallas, Texas, Liza M. Quinones continues to lead the way in financial solutions, guiding small business owners toward growth, success, and financial prosperity. Her unique selling proposition centers around a results-oriented approach, ensuring clients receive tangible, actionable steps to achieve business success.

ww.lizaquinones.com
PowerfulFemaleImmigrants.com

BANANA SPLIT CHOCOLATE SUNDAE

Anne Price, Ukraine

My story began like any other immigrant's, I suppose – coming to America full of hopes and dreams. Our stories might share commonalities, but each of us has something unique and intimate to share.

I was hungry, scared, and intimidated to enter a world completely unknown to me. Leaving behind my best friends and many family members, I embarked with my mother and father in search of a better future, carrying little clothing, no knowledge of English, and no money. Every moment on this journey was important to me and has helped shape the essence of the woman I am today. Flying across the Atlantic Ocean to the big world called America, which people referred to as the world of opportunity and wealth, we believed we would find prosperity.

I evolved from a shy and poor immigrant teenage girl facing numerous obstacles into a successful finance executive working in sunny and beautiful Hollywood, California. My story will delve into why, for me, bananas, chocolate, family, and money all assimilate with wealth and how they hold personal significance to all my achievements.

I will unveil how I slowly built success, wealth, strength, and power. In my case, perseverance, hard work, patience, gratitude, and positivity are the attributes that made it possible.

My journey began in Kyiv, Ukraine, as an innocent, pimple-faced 13-year-old who still played with dolls. I was a late bloomer, to say the least. We lived modestly on the outskirts of Kyiv as a Jewish family. My future held little promise, as being Jewish brought with it many obstacles in the Soviet Union (USSR) at the time. My dad was an engineer, and my mom was a bookkeeper. I remember it was a hot day in July when my dad announced, "We are going to America!" It was a shock to my mother and me. We were given very little notice and only allowed a small suitcase for personal belongings and sentimental items. I had to abandon my favorite doll, along with all my friends from school.

We arrived at the main train station late in the evening and were placed in an empty train cart. We had military personnel accompanying us; I didn't understand why, though I later learned it was for our protection. It didn't seem like that. No one slept that night; we were all anxious and scared.

We passed the Czech Republic and were met by more scary-looking military men, and this time, they sat with us. I wasn't very tall, maybe five feet at best, and I was petrified – it seemed to me that their guns were directed at us. Finally, we made it to Vienna, Austria, where we lived in a compound that resembled a camp or a hospital. We had no money, but we had shelter and food, so we were grateful! We met several other families on the same journey as us to the land of opportunity, America.

To ultimately make it to America, we had to travel through

multiple countries that accepted immigrants and kept them safe. This compound served as a safe house until our next destination. Vienna was beautiful and clean, with no trash anywhere. Even the asphalt was clean. The streets were lined with lush green trees, and a pleasant aroma emanated through the city.

One distinct memory I have from Vienna is of a small chocolate store on the corner from our compound. I begged my parents to let me go inside, but my dad was adamant that we couldn't enter the store because we didn't have any money. We were intimidated by all the shoppers going in and out, carrying chocolates and savoring the pleasures of every mouthful. We probably looked crazy, but all we did was stare at them through the storefront window as they indulged in the chocolatey sweetness. Then I noticed a vent connected to the store window. I was astonished by the heavenly smell of chocolate coming out of it. All I could think about was how much I wished I could taste some of that chocolate. My mouth was watering, my stomach was growling, and I couldn't move.

For the next two weeks in Vienna, I made my parents go to the same chocolate shop, stand outside by the vent, and smell the delicious scent of chocolate. My senses were overwhelmed by the beautiful aroma, but my stomach remained depleted. I thought to myself in that moment: when I got to America, I, too, would one day be able to eat chocolate in abundance like those shoppers. Childhood has a unique way of imprinting memories in our minds, and I know this vivid recollection from my immigration will be with me for a lifetime.

After about two weeks, we left Vienna by another train. This time, we didn't have any military with us; we were just surrounded by random passengers going about their business. On this train, my mother tried to speak with another lady by using her hands and speaking Russian, and in response, the lady shouted back in her own native language, Italian. Neither understood the other, many hand gestures were exchanged. The nice lady offered me a soft black stick that smelled funny; I wasn't sure what it was until I bit into it, and then I was too ashamed to spit it out. It was black licorice, and it was absolutely disgusting; it tasted bitter, like medicine. I was not impressed with Italian candy on that day.

We arrived in a small, coastal town called Ladispoli, Italy, located about two hours by train from Rome, where we gratefully accepted a kind family's hospitality. We stayed there for two months because it took some time to obtain the necessary paperwork to legally enter America. We also had to get a sponsor from America who could vouch for us.

My dad tried to earn money for us, but unfortunately, we didn't speak any Italian or English, so there wasn't much work available. My parents cleaned homes and were able to get by. We ate lots of pasta because that was all we could afford. To us, it was heavenly; we were thankful to have a roof over our heads and food on the table to share.

We would often go to a neighborhood park to walk around. One time, I saw a cart in the park that was selling fruits, ice cream, and, of course, many other things we couldn't afford. That was the first time I saw the funny yellow fruit called a banana, which I had only heard about from people's stories and the movies. Some exotic fruits were very scarce at that time in the USSR. I had imagined that the soft, sweet fruit would taste like a sugar cotton cloud. I cried hard that day, begging my parents to buy me the banana, but they did not have enough money. I never told my parents, but that day is still etched in my memory. I was so angry at the time, and I swore to myself that when I grew up, I would never deprive my children of bananas.

Two months later, we finally boarded the plane to America, arriving in Los Angeles in late September. The whole thing was a shock, a blur, and entirely overwhelming. I do remember proudly holding an American flag in my hands when we reached the airport gate, wearing Levi's jeans and a colorful tee-shirt with the words "Mexico City" across it – kind of ironic, since I didn't know what the T-shirt even said.

A generous family housed us while we got on our feet. My dad started cleaning toilets and passing out advertising flyers early in the morning. I even helped him during the week before school. My mom enrolled in school to learn English. It was a tough time, with very little food and lots of confusion. We had to find furniture from the dumpsters to use, literally. I will never forget the bright yellow 70s-style plaid loveseat; it was our proud moment—a new couch. My dad used to say, "Someone's trash is someone's treasure." How true, even to this day! I will never forget that very special time.

We all shared one room, and I had the luxury of the loveseat sofa as my bed. My school experience, where I was enrolled in ESL classes, was underwhelming academically and overwhelming in every other way. There were five different Annas in my class, all of whom spoke Spanish, so everyone assumed I spoke Spanish too. I joked that I would learn Spanish before mastering English. That year, I decided to go by "Anne" to show a little individuality. I wanted to be different, to stand out a little. I still have that spirit in me.

I was enrolled in lower-level science and math classes because of my lack of English skills, even though I was good at these subjects back home in Ukraine. In Kyiv, I was mastering Calculus and Physics, but in America, I was uninterested and bored by school academically. I remember practicing English every day in front of a mirror in the closet, next to the Scott Baio poster. I was hopeful that one day, I would be able to excel academically and take higher-level classes. That didn't really happen. By the time I went to high school, my parents were both working constantly, and my education was not their focus. They also didn't know very much about the U.S. education system. I had to be my own advocate through high school, though my grades and my English continued to be mediocre. Sometimes I wonder what would have happened if I hadn't pushed myself.

At the age of 16, I started working at a carpet store, answering telephones, which was dreadful. I was very embarrassed by my heavy accent, but I forced myself to speak, and I kept practicing in front of the mirror in my closet (my only private place) with Scott Baio smiling at me through the poster. I saw hope in his eyes. When I announced that I was going to college, my parents were surprised. I still wonder whether they didn't see my full potential or simply didn't think college was a possibility for me. I was a quiet and reserved child, often keeping to myself, and I wasn't very articulate.

In 1988, I started attending California State University, Northridge, which happened to be one of the best state universities for accounting and finance degrees. As I delved into academics and became increasingly sure of myself and my abilities, I signed up for numerous accounting and business courses and really enjoyed them. These subjects made sense to me because they were logical. I was lucky enough to befriend some people from a business society called

Beta Alpha Psi, who helped introduce me to social events and job fairs for accounting firms. Through my peers and friends on campus, I was able to get an internship at Fox Studio. I worked there for two years while in college, which was a pivotal first step in my career path.

I focused on obtaining a job in a top accounting firm when I graduated. I attended all social functions and met and introduced myself to partners and managers at these firms. I volunteered, doing tax returns and other non-profit work, to ensure I was visible. Finally, in 1992, I graduated with a Bachelor of Science in Business and Accounting. I was accepted into several national and international accounting firms, but the real cherry on top came when I was offered a position at one of the Big Six accounting and audit firms in the world. It was a very proud moment for me and my family. Who knew I would come this far?

This was only the beginning of my professional journey. I worked hard to pass the four-part CPA exam while working, conquering another challenge with perseverance, hard work, and a refusal to give up on my goals and dreams. I told myself that even if it took me a little longer than others, I would succeed. It's like the classic story of the tortoise and the hare – I always felt my friends and industry counterparts moved so much quicker in school, life, career, achievements, and up the corporate ladder. However, I'm that tortoise that gets to the finish line, no matter what.

I saw my peers in fancy cars and big houses and always wondered how they got there, how their parents got there, and how they built their wealth so effortlessly. I worked even harder because I was ambitious and had a goal. I later transitioned into the entertainment industry, where I served many of my previous clients from the firm. I realized then that making connections and building business relationships with peers was extremely important.

Through the years, I started gaining more work experience. I forced myself not to be intimidated by my accent; maybe I was not as articulate as others, but I was determined to find my voice and find my calling. Over the next few years, I spread my wings. I think I started believing in myself more and more as the years went by. I believed I could, I thought it, I envisioned it, and I manifested it. It was mind over matter. I worked incredibly hard and was passionate about my work and my contribution to businesses. I was determined to learn what I didn't know and to succeed no matter what.

Even though I still had an accent and was not as articulate as my peers, I was curious, ambitious, social, and lucky to have a great circle of supportive friends. I worked hard, had an amazing work ethic, and never stopped. I went on to work in accounting and finance roles for many major studios. Additionally, between 2008 and 2015, I consulted for numerous businesses, and found it appealing and gratifying. I found my calling in helping companies with their business needs; it was very satisfying to accomplish small projects and guide companies through building and improving their accounting and operations infrastructure from the ground up.

I later took on another endeavor and became a PMP, or Project Management Professional. With CPA and PMP certifications under my belt, I was able to uncover the areas that companies needed help with by interviewing their teams and identifying weaknesses in operational processes. Companies saw great value in my services, and I loved consulting; however, I felt my skills were underutilized and I wasn't working to my full potential. I wanted more!

Then, in late 2015, I was offered the opportunity to become a Controller for a startup production studio with only 40 employees. I took a chance on them, a very young company that didn't have much history, and luckily, they also took a chance on me. By far, this has been the career move I am most proud of. I'm currently serving as an SVP Controller at major media company. Being an executive takes a lot of hard work, perseverance, patience, resilience, and learning. It didn't happen overnight, and I had my doubts and hesitations, but I listened to my gut and intuition to lead me in the right direction. I know my worth, and I found my voice, even with that accent.

As an SVP Controller, I now oversee accounting and finance for many divisions globally, including film, tv, animation, gaming, and sports. Our media company has grown into a huge global enterprise with over 1,000 employees. We are becoming a global leader in providing content in this new, emerging market of streaming video. Even in my role as an executive, I realize I'm not an expert in every technical accounting treatment or guidance, and that is okay. I've learned to seek advice and help from my peers and colleagues when I need it. I promote a healthy team environment, mentor and encourage my colleagues and teammates to ask questions, speak their minds, collaborate on problems, and create cohesive solutions together. I believe that learning and continuing education are essential to both individual and company success.

I have successfully built an incredible team of professionals, along with a strong infrastructure in my company, by connecting the necessary software technology with the demands of the growing business. I try to provide valuable guidance to my staff and future successors. To my surprise, I was even recently nominated by my peers for a Los Angeles Business Journal Magazine Mentor of the Year Award, helping me finally realize that I am making an impact.

I was able to build not just my career but also my beautiful family. I got married and had two amazing children, Ryan and Arielle. I tried to spend as much time as possible with my children while maintaining my goal of creating a better future for them. I felt guilty for not always being at school events and for being the first person to drop them off at school in the morning and the last person to pick them up from after-school programs. I also felt guilty leaving work early at 6 pm to pick up my kids because I was potentially missing out on career opportunities. My job was very demanding, to say the least, as we worked 12- to 16-hour days. I'm not going to lie; it was tough to maintain a life/work balance in the 1990s and early 2000s. But I was determined to be able to do both and succeed.

Another obstacle presented itself in late 2006 when I got divorced. I pulled through and lived modestly while fully supporting my two children. I'm proud to say that both my kids are incredible adults now with thriving career paths. Maybe they saw a hard worker in me, even during those tough times, and were inspired – who knows?

When my kids were very young, we would drive through rich neighborhoods and admire the huge houses. Their friends were multi-generation Americans with old or existing wealth built by their parents, grandparents, and great-grandparents. They had bigger homes, nicer cars, and designer clothes. In a way, these things were a statement of success. I would always think about how important it was to create wealth, not just to feel a sense of accomplishment, but for my children, future grandchildren, and generations to come. In my opinion, generational wealth is not a prerequisite to success by any means, but it does help in many ways.

However, I always reminded myself and my kids that success and wealth are not the same thing. The essence of success is accomplishment, no matter how big or small. We must be grateful for all the small achievements we make through our life journey and strive to do better as we climb the ladder of life. That ladder can look different for everyone; it's individual. Your definition of success may differ from mine, but we all strive to be the best versions of ourselves.

I think I can say I have finally reached my success point. It comes from my family recognizing my success and being my number one cheerleader.

In the last several years, I have been able to afford a better life for myself and for my children. I'm now a proud mom of two successful children and a confident executive with a future consulting practice. I own two homes filled with nothing less than love, chocolate, and bananas. Hard work, perseverance, learning and continuing to better myself, finding my voice, and believing in myself made me the strong, powerful, and successful woman I am today. I hope to pass on the wisdom and lessons learned in my life to other aspiring young women who may also have doubt about their voices due to their background as immigrants.

I'm continuing to persevere in this country that provided me the opportunity, and I'm not about to stop. This tortoise keeps on moving.

Now, it's time to really enjoy that banana split chocolate sundae with a cherry on top!

Anne Price

Anne Price, a seasoned CPA, is a remarkable trailblazer in the entertainment industry. With a career spanning over three decades, she has not only established herself as a financial expert but also as a passionate advocate for diversity, mentorship, elder care, and making a meaningful impact in society.

Having arrived in the United States from Ukraine, Anne's journey has been one of resilience and determination. Her early experiences as an immigrant fueled her drive to succeed, and she swiftly rose through the ranks in the entertainment finance sector. Today, she holds a prominent executive position at a leading media company.

Anne's expertise extends far beyond traditional accounting. She is renowned for her ability to provide technical accounting consulting services and build robust business systems infrastructures for companies in various business sectors. Her contributions have transformed financial operations, ensuring that businesses operate efficiently and effectively.

As a mentor, Anne has played an instrumental role in shaping the careers of aspiring professionals in the industry. She is a tireless advocate for diversity and inclusion, education, and financial well-being for senior members of the community.

Despite her demanding career, Anne is a devoted mother of two children, balancing the demands of motherhood with her professional responsibilities. She firmly believes in setting an example for her children, demonstrating the value of hard work, compassion, and giving back to society.

Anne's passion for mentoring young professionals, technical expertise, and commitment to building strong communities underline her mission to leave a lasting impact on society at large.

linktr.ee/anneprice

PowerfulFemaleImmigrants.com

JOURNEY TO VIEN'S SELF-DISCOVERY

Vien Nguyen, Vietnam

In 1996, My family and I had the opportunity to come to America to pursue the American Dream of financial freedom and access to educational opportunities. My mother took the leap of faith and move to America with all her kids in pursuing her children's happiness.

My mother used to work two jobs to support her four children, and because of this, my siblings and I hardly saw her. Knowing that my mother worked extremely hard in her life, I was determined at a young age to go to college, obtain a degree, and be extremely successful. I wanted to help my mother retire early, enjoy her retirement age and support my siblings so they could pursue their dreams.

I attended the University of Colorado at Boulder and earned a BS/MS in chemical engineering. I have been working in the oil and gas industry for the past 12 years as a facilities engineer/project engineer. Besides working in the oil and gas industry, I also actively and passively invest in real estate in pursuing the financial freedom and generational wealth to gain more time with my beloved daughter. To date, I own 700+ units in apartment complexes as both a limited partner and a general partner. As a general partner, I support the property management and asset management for all the assets that we own in the Midwest area.

The primary reason that I ventured into the real estate investment world is because of my daughter. My daughter is 5-year old. She is my everything, young, smart, and beautiful; I love her dearly and want to spend as much time with her as possible in her growing years. I enjoy exploring different places with her every weekend, like the museum, park, play dates, etc. Each time I visit my properties in other states, I take her with me to show her what I do and why I do it. Because of my daughter, I am extremely passionate about the entrepreneurship world and am actively pursuing opportunities to permanently transition into real estate and entrepreneurship and become my own boss and to gain back tim and be with my daughter.

Things were heading the way I planned in my life as I worked in the W2 world while simultaneously investing in real estate. I was planning to slowly transition into the real estate investing world, but several events unexpectedly happened and they forever altered my life. Little did I know, these changes were for the better because they allowed me to undergo a major discovery and transformation in order for me to find my true identity.

In 2020, my mother and my family moved to Dallas, Texas, to be closer to real estate investors so I could pursue my dreams. I established many great relationships with real estate partners and invested in several multifamily investments while in Dallas. My family was doing extremely well and we were moving along our intended path.

In July 2021, however, when my mother fell ill, I was left alone in Dallas to take care of her – all while still raising my then three-years old daughter. Due to the severity of my mother's health, my daughter, my mother, and I moved back to Colorado in July of 2021 so my siblings could be near our mother in the hopes that she would recover quickly. On March 3rd, 2022, the moment that changed my life forever. I left the hospital around 5 a.m. that day, and my mother's heart was still beating even though she was unconscious. At 6 a.m., I received a phone call from my dear brother, who was at the hospital. He told me that our mom was in critical condition, and I should head back to the hospital as soon as possible. Upon my arrival, I learned that my mother had already passed by the time my brother called, but he didn't have the courage to say so over the phone. I had lost my best friend and my beloved mother forever. My mother was the only one who had always been there with me and supported me unconditionally.

As I went through the healing process, I listened to a lot of motivational videos and inspirational speakers like Brian Tracey, TD Jakes, Toby Robbins, etc. but I continued to run into more roadblocks as the saying said, "When it rains, it pours." I went through a divorce while my mother was ill, my most trusted real estate partner announced that he was quitting from multifamily real estate investment in early May 2023, and my dad passed away unexpectedly later that same month.

My world turned upside-down in May 2023; I will never forget this period in life. All these events happening simultaneously put me in a deep state of shock and stress. Additionally, it was to the point where I underwent a major self-discovery journey. Everything I thought I knew before was no longer with me or part of my identity and I felt so lost in life. As I sought answers through God's teaching, meditation, and listening to motivational/inspirational videos, I learned one invaluable lesson: although I thought I was successful and had everything I wanted, I was never focused on myself, my personal well-being, my daughter, and my happiness and the bottom line was, I did not take care of myself first while I was putting my work, family, and building wealth ahead of my well-being.

The two favorite books that help me to work on my personal development and discover my identity are Miracle Morning and Breaking the Habit of Being Yourself. I also have broken away from negative people and only surrounded myself with many great individuals who share the same values, work ethics, and visions as we help each other reach those goals by getting 1% better every day. I am grateful to be part of the MIH community, where I met people who supported me unconditionally through the lowest time in my life and they also stepped in to help me manage and reposition our real estate assets. Even though a few letdown partners withdrew investments and didn't honor their commitments, my real estate investment journey remained fruitful and promising. Those experiences merely taught me to find more valuable partners in the future and how to ensure their compatibility.

I also surround myself with powerful female immigrants who stand strong among each other and lift each other's spirits up so we can be the best version of ourselves. We discuss our life lessons, daily routines and betterment, business ideas, and how to stay focused on our goals. Through this Powerful Female Immigrant network, I also gained knowledge of entrepreneurship and positive mindset development. I feel extremely blessed and grateful to be surrounded by these amazing individuals from both my real estate investments and my powerful female immigrant groups.

From the beginning, the tragic events in my life had driven me to the brink of deep depression. However, these events were also a blessing in disguise because they have pushed me outside my comfort zone. The new adventure I took on were, in fact, extremely uncomfortable, things I never could have imagined, but they were also life changing.

The lessons I have learned have helped me become a better, and stronger individual for my future endeavors. I have learned how to find a quality partner, whether in business or in personal life. My future partners must have integrity and honesty, a strong sense of commitment and family-oriented, and demonstrate that their actions speak louder their words. I have learned the importance of self-love, self-care, and self-development, as I must be happy first before taking care of anyone else. Previously, my emotions have impacted my decision-making skill, and I need to learn how to use logics over all emotions when making major decisions.

Through my personal trials and tribulations, working in the corporate world, and pursuing real estate investments, I have finally discovered my true "why" – what I want to do and where I want to be in life. My "WHY" is truly my daughter and time freedom. I must focus on future endeavors that have the most positive impact on both of us because at the end of the day, I want to have the time and financial freedom to be an active part of my daughter's life.

I am extremely passionate when it comes to real estate investments, entrepreneurship ideas, people motivation, and exploring different ideas to build wealth. I want to be near a group of entrepreneurs who work together to build wealth, push each other toward financial freedom, and, more importantly, want to have a support system based on common goals. As the saying goes, we are stronger as a team, and with the right team, we can achieve anything. I want to slowly transition from W2 into full-time entrepreneurship and investing worlds. I want to work on my own schedule and time so I can have the freedom to be with my daughter.

As I continue to pursue these adventures while being the best mother to my daughter, I must remind myself that my daughter deserves the best from the moment she first stepped into this world. In addition to surrounding myself with positive and powerful individuals, I practice these daily routines to stay focused and in the moment: morning prayers, meditation, affirmation, and feeling happiness when I wake up my daughter every morning. These daily routines have helped me find myself and determine my goals for the future. My goal in 1-3 years is to become the person that I dream of being, as well as to be free from the corporate world. If any of these stories resonate with you, let's connect, discuss our experiences, and share any tips that will better our lives (see the link below). I'm currently working on my transformation website, which will be launched in early 2024. Thank you for taking the time to read about my journey and experience. I would love to meet you and connect one day.

Vien Nguyen

Vien has a BS/MS in Chemical Engineering from the University of Colorado at Boulder in 2010. She has been working in the oil & gas industry for the past 12+ years as facilities engineer/project manager, managing projects ranging from $200K - $15MM from conceptual to construction/operation.

Upon graduation, Vien began investing in SFH passively by using buy/hold/sell model while working her day job. In late 2020, Vien began transitioning into large multifamily investment due to the economy of scale and to build generational of wealth for her family and her daughter. By leveraging her oil & gas experience over the past 11 years, she uses these skillsets and specializes in the deal analysis/underwriting and asset management to ensure these multifamily investments are meeting the investment business plans. To date, Vien, invests in 800 units+ spanning multiple states: TX, NC, SD, OH, PA and OK.

Vien is the Chief Operation Officer at Meliorem Capital, specializing in assess management, business execution, and ensure the day-to-day operations are meeting the company objectives and goals to provide the most economical returns to the investors.

Outside of Meliorem Capital and her oil & gas day job, she enjoys spending quality time with her four years old daughter by taking her to many different places (swimming, museum, tennis, hiking, and outdoor activities).

VienLegacy.com

PowerfulFemaleImmigrants.com

YOU'RE DIVORCED, NOW WHAT?

Ngoc T. Tran, Vietnam

Accept yourself with all your faults and glories
Release yourself from your sad and lonely stories
Bring back those youthful days and nights
Ignite your fires' delights
The passions locked within
Once more released without a doubt
Recapture what life is all about
--Ngoc T. Tran

So, you have gone through a divorce...now what? If you were to research online, you would find that the divorce rate in the United States for 2022 is estimated to be from 30% to 50% for first marriages. Rates of divorce increase for second marriages, standing somewhere between 60% and 67%, and are even higher for third marriages. These statistics seem to hold true in my own personal experiences as well. My parents separated when I was a teenager. Of my seven siblings and myself, half of us had our first marriages end in divorce; currently, only one among us has decided to remarry. Tracking rates of divorce by ethnicity (Asian, Black, Hispanic, Caucasian, etc.), we see that Asians have the lowest rates of divorce. The most typical reasons for divorce can vary but often include financial strain, infidelity, and communication problems, among other factors; all this holds true among my siblings and me.

Being raised in an Asian immigrant family, the idea of divorce was foreign to us. Our upbringing emphasized the value of prioritizing family, fostering unconditional love for our children, and navigating through all challenges, even if it involved coping with betrayal. We were instilled with the belief that our personal desires should be set aside for the betterment of the family unit.

Frequently, we end up sacrificing our individual identities because we prioritize the needs, ambitions, and desires of others over our own. From a young age, we were ingrained with traditional role expectations: women were primarily tasked with domestic duties, while men were expected to handle outdoor tasks and manage finances. As women, we were instructed to communicate only when addressed first, implying our opinions held little value. We were "programmed" to prove our worthiness and "made to believe" that we needed to work twice as hard to earn equivalent pay. This kind of conditioning often leads to a loss of self-prioritization, personal identity, and happiness.

As Vietnamese refugees, "boat people" living in San Francisco from 1979 to 1988, my family grappled with the constraints of poverty. We arrived in the U.S. with just ten dollars in our pocket and the clothes on our backs. After 24 years of marriage, my father decided to live separately from my mother and us. He drove our family from San Francisco to Beaumont, Texas, home to my mother's siblings, and returned to live with my third eldest brother. My second eldest brother had left home and joined the Air Force. This left my mother to bear the financial and emotional burdens of raising six children, aged between eight and twenty-one, without any financial support from my father. Despite her struggles as a single parent, when we were children, my mother never criticized my father for his shortcomings, alcoholism, infidelities, or gambling problems, which often impeded his ability to provide for us financially.

In our youth, we were oblivious to the hardship of life; it was normal. Our mother juggled multiple jobs, sewing garments for small local clothing factories in the evenings and working at a shrimp factory when the boats came in teeming with shrimp. After school, my siblings and I would join her, beheading shrimps for two dollars a bucket. We would return home with smelly dollar bills, which we would wash in the machine and then carefully iron. The money we earned was handed over to our mother to pay the mortgage and groceries; that was our reality for close to two years until that fateful day when our home was destroyed in a fire caused by electrical issues while we were in school.

Following the fire, the state of our uninhabitable house forced us to take refuge in a hotel. Any personal items that had not been consumed by the fire fell prey to thieves. However, this unforeseen fire came as a disguised blessing. The insurance settlement provided us with the means to fly back to San Francisco and start anew.

My mother enrolled herself in vocational school and secured a job as a social worker. Her meticulousness, friendly demeanor, and professional conduct caught the eye of her manager, who then recommended her for a dental assistant position at her son's dental office. This job, combined with the after-school jobs my siblings and

I held, transformed our family's circumstances, enabling my mother to secure a far improved lifestyle for us compared to living in Texas.

The failure of my parent's marriage served as a reality check on my relationship with my former husband. In every partnership, the lovely moments etched early on are expected to give sustenance during the challenging later years. Being in love blinds us to our partner's flaws, as we find excuses to rationalize them primarily because of our belief in their inherent kindness and the hope that they will eventually transform into the people we wish they would be. My ex-husband's unexpected betrayal after nearly fifteen years of marriage left me bewildered as to why he renounced our marital commitments, fundamental principles, and Asian customs.

The birth of our son changed me as I embraced the multiple roles of mother, wife, caregiver, homemaker, professional worker, and all-around "super mom." As time continued, monotony set in; every day resembled its predecessor. Immersed in the relationship, I lost my self-identity, living passively without acknowledging the dysfunction of our marriage until it was officially over.

Divorce is an emotional whirlwind, with each partner holding on to their narratives of perceived truths. Regrettably, divorce reveals a darker side in some of us, sparking disputes over asset distribution, finances, child custody, pets, and even trivial matters. The vindictiveness within seizes control, greed, and the urge "to be right," coupled with a dominating ego, overrides the rational consideration of what truly is fair and just. Thousands or even hundreds of thousands of dollars are squandered on lawyer fees, custody battles, and equitable division of possessions.

Despite the emotional turmoil, my commitment to ensuring a secure future for my teenage son and myself guided me to avoid unnecessary disputes over the division of assets and finances. We employed a paralegal, and after a six-year process, our divorce was finalized, costing us merely $1,200 in charges.

In many ways, the divorce turned out to be a hidden blessing. I had learned from my mother to never relinquish total financial control to a partner, leading to us maintaining separate bank accounts along with one joint account for investments. This arrangement granted me the freedom and flexibility I needed to leave my marital home and start my healing journey.

The initial months of being a single parent supporting a teenager were incredibly challenging. Guilt washed over me for not having flexible working hours or being at home when my son returned from middle school. I was unable to eat or sleep and lost thirty pounds in just three months. Emotional tears would catch me off guard, whether during my commute, at work, or at completely random moments. Seeking comprehension amidst the chaos, I delved into inspirational videos, self-help books and engaged with sound healers, emotional therapists, massage therapists, and acupuncturists. This journey of healing led me to prioritize self-love, cherish my time with my son, and gradually progress as a single mother.

As overwhelmed as I was emotionally, mentally, and spiritually both during the marriage and through the divorce, I am thankful for the wisdom I gained and, most importantly, the precious gift of my son. Had I remained married, I would not have become the person I am today: someone who positively influences others' personal and business finances and someone who could find love anew with my soulmate, who resonates with my core values and beliefs.

If you knew that you only had a year, a month, a week, or even a day left to live, would your actions differ, or would you choose to continue living in a marriage that fails to fill your heart with happiness and joy? Would you prefer to endure a life tormented by dread of the unknown, silently bearing regrets, allowing the prospect of living a more fulfilling life to slip away?

I chose to walk away and build the life I was intended to live, filled with love, joy, passion, and purpose. I am divorced. So what? Now what?

NEW DIRECTIONS

Free your mind from the worries and the pains
Release the controls upon your brain
For the possibilities will be uncontained
Your visions will be unreined
Nothing will be so plain
Colors will rearrange
Your life will realign
With the new visions in mind
New goals redefined
New directions and steps you will find
New hopes and dreams so profound
Your life energy will be divine
And your mind once more refined
--Ngoc T. Tran

Ngoc T. Tran

Ngoc T. Tran is a Certified Public Accountant, debt, wealth, and business strategist, global business connector, impact speaker, 2x international bestselling author, and the host of *The Paradigm Shifters Show* on Boss Ladies TV Network. As CEO and founder of JJ Capital Partners, Ngoc is passionate about helping people understand the value of time and money by sharing strategies for creating multiple streams of residual income and providing solutions for shifting people's financial paradigms.

Ngocttran.com

PowerfulFemaleImmigrants.com

NORTH STAR - THE GUIDING LIGHT

Wilette Nguyen, Philippines

The Journey

My journey began on March 21, 1978, in Laoag City, Philippines. I was the fourth child, born an American citizen because my father was a United States Marine. I was an American citizen, something I didn't realize was so valuable until my adult life.

In 1982, at the age of four, I immigrated to Northern California. My parents and older siblings had immigrated three years earlier to start building a life for us. For my mother and father, this meant finding a place to call home, securing jobs, and establishing a safe, loving environment for my siblings and me to grow up in.

Northern California became the family's forever home, where I would grow up, explore my passions, seek adventures, and build the foundation of my life story. We moved around a lot during the first few years before settling in the suburbs. The suburbs provided a nurturing and safe environment for us. I felt a strong sense of community and family, something I hadn't felt or seen before (aside from TV). The suburbs would be where I would grow up, make lifelong friends, meet my husband (the ultimate North Star), and eventually go back to build my own home and raise my children.

As I journeyed through middle and high school in the suburbs, I felt a sense of belonging.

I immersed myself in my friendships and student life and enjoyed all the opportunities that came my way. I have the fondest memories of those times, and even now, thinking about them makes me smile.

Though my undergraduate life may not have been as exciting as my friends' journeys to dream schools and studying abroad, I took pride in the choices I made. I knew I had to put myself through school, so I opted for a state university close to home so I could balance school and a full-time job.

Throughout my undergraduate years, I navigated the challenges that came with that balance. At one point, I couldn't do it anymore, and I had to take some time off to work full-time. This decision caused my path to graduation to stretch beyond my initial expectations. But these hurdles only served to strengthen my resolve to succeed. In the end, I persevered and received my bachelor's degree in sociology, a testament to my determination to obtain the first college diploma in my family.

The North Stars

The early years of my career were characterized by a search for my true passion and purpose. I started out working in public health, but I determined very quickly that it was not my calling. I struggled to separate my emotions from the cases I worked on and often came home with a sense of guilt and sadness thinking about the people I had encountered that day. Then I went into corporate America and found that I thrived in that environment, but not in the positions I had taken. So, I made it my mission to find where I would fit in.

North Star 1

It was in my mid-twenties that I encountered my first North Star, US. As the CFO of the company I worked for, US was an educated and experienced, as well as a tough, no-nonsense leader (a characteristic he attributes to his time in the Israeli army). US took me under his wing, recognizing my potential and offering his invaluable mentorship.

Under US's guidance, I learned the power of education and the importance of reading. Every meeting with him began with the question, "What are you reading?" He had an insatiable appetite for knowledge that he got from reading. He was intelligent and wise, and I found myself in awe of him. His mentorship ignited a fire within me to pursue further education, ultimately leading me to earn my master's degree in business.

North Star 2

The journey didn't end there. I discovered my second North Star, JW. JW was being recruited to be the CEO of the company I worked for, and his arrival was transformative. JW was not only brilliant, but he was also a kind and empathetic leader – a leadership style polar opposite to that of US, which intrigued me. He nurtured my growth and instilled in me the confidence to believe in myself and my abilities. With his encouragement, I began to realize that there was nothing I couldn't achieve, something he often reminded me with a resounding, "Yes, you can." To this day, whether personal or professional, I remind myself amid self-doubt, "Yes, you can." With the people I mentor or who work on my teams, I also mimic those exact words just as JW did to me in his nurturing and calming manner: "Yes, you can."

JW played a significant role in building the foundation of the leader I aspired to become. As my career developed and transitioned under his watchful eye, I matured both professionally and personally. It was through JW that I would meet my third North Star, JPS. I still remember the day before entering JPS's office when JW looked at me and said, "I've taken you as far as I could. The rest is up to you now." At that moment, I knew I held the reins of my destiny.

North Star 3 - Polaris

JPS became my first female role model and mentor, an influential figure who would shape my future in immeasurable ways. JPS was the president in a multi-billion-dollar public company and one of Forbes Magazine's Most Influential Women in Tech. It was JPS who became the guiding light, showing me what a powerful woman is and can achieve.

Our relationship evolved from an employee-manager dynamic into a powerful partnership based on mutual respect and admiration. JPS was everything I desired to be. Her belief in me shifted my mindset from "I should" to "I deserve," reminding me that hard work and dedication indeed pay off.

Under JPS's leadership, I felt empowered and supported to explore my potential within the organization. She encouraged me to take on challenges, exposed me to invaluable experiences, and connected me with influential people.

I could do anything with JPS behind me, and I did. I moved through the organization quickly; with every achievement came a promotion, and with every promotion came trust and acknowledgment from other senior leaders in the organization. I have led offices around the world, overseeing global expansion and actively engaging with federal, state, and local agencies to represent the organization. I articulated its mission and vision while striving to achieve its ambitious goals. The sky was truly the limit.

Through JPS' guidance, I grew as an individual and a leader, and eventually, I became a mentor to others. She also ignited my aspirations to pursue executive programs and continue my education at prestigious institutions like Oxford, Cornell, and Northeastern, where I continued my self-development journey.

North Star 4

The guidance of my North Stars continued to shape my life. SG, introduced to me by JW, became another influential mentor and one of my best friends today. SG was a true master of using facts and data to navigate business challenges. I learned from SG to respect the power of evidence and utilize it as my ammunition when faced with complex situations. Armed with facts and data, I learned to prove theories, validate hypotheses, and convince others to act. I didn't know then, but what SG taught me would help me face one of the biggest and scariest challenge of my life – cancer.

Battling Cancer - A Test of Resilience and Strength

In 2021, life took an unexpected turn. Diagnosed with Stage 2 breast cancer not once but twice that year, I found my world turned upside down. It was undoubtedly the toughest year I had ever faced, navigating through grueling chemotherapy, surgeries, and the emotional toll on both me and my family.

In the face of this adversity, I made a firm decision to retain as much control as possible. I devoured knowledge on cancer (using data and facts I discovered through my research as ammunition against my fight with cancer), continued to work through the treatment, and maintained a positive outlook (or at least tried). I became determined to fight the battle with resilience and strength. But it was not easy, and at times I failed. I masked the pain and the struggle; I hid the tears. Cancer took a lot from me. I struggled with brain fog, forgetfulness, not being mentally sharp, and feeling like I was losing my mind (intelligence). I even had one man say to me, "Now that you don't have your looks, what are you going to do?" At that moment, I second-guessed myself – all the hard work, my achievements, and my self-worth.

It took time to recover, heal, and build a new me (yes, a new me) after the treatments were done and I was deemed cancer-free.

Rebuilding Confidence and Wellness

During my cancer battle, I encountered another North Star, ES, whose guidance proved instrumental in my recovery. ES emphasized the importance of rebuilding confidence and prioritizing wellness during challenging times. She was going through her own battles, so together, we supported each other. "We can together" became the motto. I learned to lean on the power of (the WeShred) community and support, recognizing that I was not alone in my journey.

The Power of Hope and Connection

Through the (WeShred) community ES provided, I discovered another guiding light, North Star, AOB. Through AOB's mentorship and friendship, I learned about the significance of hope and connection. AOB and I are forever connected in our journey with cancer, hers with her mother. The strength and resilience I drew from this meaningful relationship fortified my resolve to overcome the obstacles that cancer placed in my path. AOB not only gave me hope and connection, but she also give others diagnosed with cancer the power of hope and connection through The Chemo Club.

The Power of Partnership

My husband, PN, has been my unwavering support and the ultimate North Star since the day he entered my life. Without his constant encouragement and belief in me, my journey and story wouldn't have been as empowering or successful. His love and drive have been the guiding force behind my achievements, reminding me to reach for the stars and never settle for less. Through him, I understand the strength of partnership, and together, we have embraced its power.

The Unbreakable Spirit of a Powerful Female Immigrant

The guidance of my North Stars and the resilience I developed during my cancer battle culminated in a transformation that redefined me as a powerful female immigrant. I learned that empowerment, success, and inspiration were not just about professional achievements but also about embracing challenges with courage. They are about instilling the belief that everyone is capable of greatness. Everyone.

The Legacy of Empowerment

Looking back on my life's journey, I can confidently say that empowerment is a gift that keeps on giving. When one person is empowered, they have the capacity to empower countless others, creating a ripple effect of positive change. I often think about the impact my North Stars had on my life and their profound influence on the trajectory of my success.

In this book, *Powerful Female Immigrants*, my story is just one of many that exemplify the strength, resilience, and determination of immigrant women who have overcome obstacles to achieve greatness. Each of these women carries within her a North Star, a guiding force that propels her forward on the path to empowerment and success.

The North Star, with its unwavering and constant presence in the night sky, has long served as a guiding beacon for travelers seeking direction. In the same way, my North Stars have been my constant guides, illuminating my path and showing me the way when I needed it most. They have taught me that empowerment comes not just from within but from the collective support and belief of those around us.

As I continue my journey, I strive to be a North Star for others, offering guidance, support, and inspiration to those who need it most. Just as the North Star has been my unwavering guide, I aspire to empower others to embrace their full potential and chase their dreams fearlessly.

My story as a powerful female immigrant is a testament to the strength of the human spirit and the transformative effects of empowerment. It is a story of resilience, confidence, and the unyielding pursuit of success. Through the guidance of my North Stars, I have found my true purpose, and I hope that my journey serves as an inspiration to all those who seek empowerment and strive to make a positive impact on the world. Let us all embrace our inner North Star, guiding us to greatness and lighting the way for others along the path of empowerment.

Wilette Nguyen

Wilette Nguyen is a highly accomplished and influential business operations executive with over 15 years of experience in leading organizations to success. With a strong educational background, Wilette holds both a bachelor's degree in sociology and master's degree in business, having further honed her expertise through executive programs at prestigious institutions like Oxford and Cornell. Currently, Wilette is pursuing her passion for law at Northeastern University School of Law.

Beyond her professional achievements, Wilette is deeply committed to empowering others. She has been a dedicated mentor and coach, guiding aspiring professionals to reach their full potential. As an advocate for gender equality, Wilette is particularly passionate about empowering women to break barriers and achieve the seemingly impossible. Through her journey as an immigrant, she has become a beacon of inspiration, motivating countless individuals to embrace their unique paths and chase their dreams with unwavering determination.

To learn more about Wilette or connect with her:

linktr.ee/wilettenguyen

PowerfulFemaleImmigrants.com

BLOOM WHEREVER YOU ARE PLANTED

Evelin Marsh, El Salvador

My name is Evelin Marsh and I am an artist, designer and optometrist from San Salvador, El Salvador. I moved to the USA in 2005 with $1000 and 75 pounds of El Salvadorian cheese. I laugh when I write that because it sounds so simple, but the true story was one of hard work, resilience and an undying love for my son.

As a young woman in my twenties in El Salvador, I had studied to be an optometrist. I start with $375.00 that was my last check working as a software support in one of the biggest banks in my country. With that money I bought 2 dozens of contact color lenses which I sold-out. Furthermore, that was my investment to open a kiosk in a big mall. 6 months after that finally I opened an Optical Business in San Salvador. Pass forward I got pregnant and turn into single mother by choice and I will chose that a hundred times.

During my pregnancy my mom was a very strong support. My pregnancy was very hard and my business sells come down 85%. That was that momentum when I can say "YOUR HARDER

TIMES YOUR BEST TIME" I struggled to find clients and pay bills. I was a member of a bank that's only for Dr. Where my credit line was in red. The investors of the Bank cited me to talk about how I can pay my CC bills that I owe (C43,750) $5K . The main investor start asking me what I can do (what was my gift) To whom I response: "I can pay if I only have a company willing to allow me to perform eye exams and optical service to all the employees and discount it from payroll" right after my answer He ask me "Do you know who we are in the real life? I have so much pain just to stand in front of them that moment that I didn't think too much who I was talking to, he was the president and director of the bigger hospital for kids in El Salvador by that time So he keep talking and he make a commitment with the others Drs. In the room that they will allow me to perform my services in every single hospital in town. I canvassed the local hospitals seeking relationships that would bring me clients. After all that I was one of the first Optical company starting mobile or express clinics to every company in my country. After much hard work and relationship building, I was able to sign up various hospitals and provided over 5000 eye exams. So grateful Business was looking up!

Fortunately, my son was born healthy, and I worked to manage both my business and the demands of solo parenting. However, the absence of my family support system was hard and made me question the idea of home. Meanwhile, my father and sisters had immigrated to Oregon, but I could not join them as they had a family VISA petition from my Aunt Lucia and I didn't qualify as I was over the legal age.

During the Santa Ana Volcano eruption happens that night, at home, with my son sleeping on the floor and the lights flickering on and off, with earthquake in sirens in the distance, I made the hard choice to leave everything I knew behind in search of a better life.

The next months were a blur as I struggled to figure out how I could manage a move to the United States while keeping my business afloat and my son safe and sound. With the big earthquake and volcanic eruption of Santa Ana all occurred during this time and there was a famine in El Salvador.

Meanwhile my son Rudy was going to pre-kinder, one day, I got a note under my business door saying: "PAY $25 A DAY TO OPEN YOUR BUSINESS OR WE WILL KIPNAP YOUR SON. WE WILL SEND OUR PEOPLE IN ONE **WEEK**.", plus the Inflation drove food prices up and the city I grew up in seemed less and less safe as a place to raise my son, all this really pushed me to make my move out of my country with my son. Thank God, we both have an American Visa because I used to travel for business before I got pregnant.

I used all my connections to gain an introduction to a doctor in San Francisco who needed an optometrist to provide eye exams for his Latin patient population. With the hope of a new job, I sold all the equipment from my optical business and I was able to save $1000. My sisters lent me money for one way plane tickets to San Francisco and I used some of my savings to purchase Salvadoran cheese to sell upon my arrival for at least to double my money. The cheese cost was $4 I sold it for $8 to $10.

Those first weeks in San Francisco, I hustled to get on my feet. I would wake up at 5am and take my son, and the cheeses I had brought with me, my uncle Saul my mom's brother welcome us in his Richmond home. Before the city was awake we drove with my uncle, I would walk around The Mission St. from restaurant to restaurant, selling my special cheese at a premium. Each round of cheese sold was one step closer to getting us started in our life in the United States.

I began to work for the Doctor as his Optometrist providing eye exams, much as I had in El Salvador. I lived with my uncle outside the city and brought my son to work with me every day. After a few weeks, I realized that my son, now 4 years old, needed to be in school. I applied for him to be in the Head start program in San Francisco, but the wait list was a mile long and I knew I couldn't bring him to work with me forever.

Soon my sisters invited me to Oregon for Christmas and I gladly accepted their invitation. Our first time in Oregon was Christmas 25th that day we saw the snow and play around well without gloves it was painful at the end. One day, my son and I were walking to the store when suddenly a woman came up to me, telling me something emphatically in English. I didn't speak a word, but understood she wanted me to follow her across the street. She led me to a school where a Spanish speaking employee was able to explain that they were a head-start school and Rudy would be able to enroll right away. And just like that, I made the decision to move to Oregon- closer to my family and where my son would be in school.

Rudy had a rough transition into the school system. I am so grateful to the Head start organization for all their support during that time. I started volunteering in the class. We were the only Latino family but there were Hindu families, African Americans and more. I felt fortunate to be part of a group of dedicated mothers helping their children assimilate into the United States and learning the language.

My sisters, my dad and I all moved into a house together. I began cleaning houses and working in a small bar in Portland as a waitress. My VISA had expired and I was here illegally but with my son in school, I chose to take the chance to stay and give him an opportunity to achieve the American dream.

With the little money that I was earning, I enrolled in Portland Community College and began studying. I studied English. Up until that point, I couldn't speak any English at all.

I worked under the table, bussing tables and in the kitchen of restaurants while I tried to grasp the English language.

My only goal was to give my son the best life possible, taking English classes together and going to the library. I was able to learn enough English to get my driver's license, offering me a freedom I had never had before.

At the restaurant, the back of the house staff- the dishwashers, cooks, bussers, there were 10 of us, we had formed an informal saving program called Tandas. Every pay check, each of us would put $100 into the fund. We each had a number for the week we would be the recipient of the fund. My number was 4.

On my week, I was given $1000 and with that money, I purchased my first ever car, a 1991 Toyota Tercel, in 2006.

I was in full survival mode. I couldn't work as an optometrist in Oregon because everyone spoke English. My education, work experience and professional acumen were lost in translation. I worked as a busgirl at a casual dining experience.

Furthermore, a friend introduced me to a woman who needed a chauffeur and recommended me for the job. She was a widow of a wealthy Man in Texas and moved to Portland. She lived off her inheritance. After she saw my work and loyalty sooner she made me her Right Hand in charge of everything in her house. She always had my best interests at heart and strived to make many introductions within her circle.

Soon after I met my biggest mentor who though me many things like home design and reinforced me to keep my English classes. I stop working at the restaurants and start working as a general manager in construction Jobs. Where my passion for design houses and construction started. I was working with my mentor during weekends early and finish very late at nights like 1:00 Am. We were a great team working remodeling houses by 2008 during the housing market crash. I was excited to learn more every day for me by this time I have learned enough English to work as his translator, I share with him how to work with Latin people and he started loving the culture and hard work that we all bring to the job site, I began learning about home construction, managing projects throughout various stages and learning on the job experience, truly acting as a handyman and working with my hands to install toilets, light fixtures, and more.

I discovered I had a true passion for home design, partially inspired by my own need to create a safe and beautiful home for my son. Once again, I went back to Portland Community College and studied project management, eventually securing my contractor license -CCB. This field offered me an opportunity to bridge the world I came from with the world I had just joined. Month by month, my English was quickly improving, and I found that my ability to manage the construction teams in Spanish and translate our progress to the English speaking heads of the company provided me a unique window into both worlds. Eventually, I negotiated my CCB license with my mentor and he gave me partial ownership of the construction company. He trust me as a person and after all my hard work, we worked together long hours during our weekends to bring the new rentals ready to listed. As we completed projects and put the houses up for sale with my own designs that was hitting the market with prices from $750.00 to $1.5M. I began to focus more on interior design that's when I found the best part Heritage School of Interior Designers in the Northwest, that was my second place that I learned a lot and my dream was a reality. I would work with staging companies to create the perfect home for potential clients. In my free time, when I wasn't working construction or spending time with my son, I began to paint. My first canvasses were a play of color and light, inspired by the landscapes in El Salvador. I remember timidly hanging them on the wall for a home about to hit the market. Later, as clients filed through the home during an open house, I was thrilled to hear positive comments about my work. After a few meetings my artwork was in Clinics, Real Estates offices, Staging Homes, and solo art shows in town.

I opened my first art show IN 2016 at Sotheby's in Lake Oswego where I sold over $5000 in artwork.

All through this time, I focused my time and energy on ensuring that my son was thriving. I was able to move him into one of the top school districts and continued to be an active volunteer in his life. He inspired me to believe anything was possible. Fast forward, my son Rudy moves to Florida Tech to study his college education as an engineer.

The moment of Eye Opening-Empty Nestled

As a mother and wife by that time, my focus was my husband and my son literally, my family. I felt that I worked hard to keep my family united at certain point and suddenly, one day you wake up and there is only you. I discovered that we need to evolve and find our own persona again. I started redesign myself and supporting other women's in the same situation without saying what I was experience. I start transforming my artwork in Textiles and making a group of women in Latin America to bring my artwork alive. Every artisan that we work with, are single mothers or moms with family working every day to BE the support in theirs families. My journey till this moment taught me that is better to teach how to fish instead giving the fish just because we have the resources. This way I build my brand "Evelin Marsh Art and Designs" where by now I have collectors of my wearable art like shoes, handbags, wallets, scarf and more is coming soon. After all this time I found my strength back again in collaboration with other women in the same transition. Before all that I learned I have a friend that was God's angel, she always was praying for me and teaching me how to pray and because God always is present in our daily life I'm assure that you are reading this not because I'm trying to impress no one but a way for you to realize the strength and the value that you have is not coming from another human been, actually is coming from your inside. With all this blooming I made connections to go to represent my artwork outside of Oregon. My first art show was in San Diego 135 artist, after that I went to New York where by now my artwork is being represented by a Gallery in Manhattan. With more hard work pushing all my strength during hard times I'm managing to go as a Gallery this time to Miami Art Basel by December 2023 which is the bigger art show in Miami. By now my son graduated from OSU College as an engineer in Computer sciences. Yes!!!! We made it, hard work from Rudy and his now Dad, the best team work as a family.

The best I can share is this: "It's not exactly what happens to us, It's the way how we left everything affect us" God never give us something bigger than our capacity of endurance.

Throughout my journey, I had several pillars of belief that kept me moving forward when times were tough. The first was to always HAVE FAITH. I knew when I moved to the United States that it was the right decision for me and my son. I didn't know how things would work out, but I was confident that God had a plan for me. However, no amount of Faith can help you achieve your goals if you are not standing with your eyes open to see the opportunities in front of you.

The Second Pillar of my beliefs is to GET READY AND OPEN TO THE OPPORTUNITY. Whether it was the opportunity to join a group to allow me to purchase a car or the opportunity to meet with my mentor that taught me how to work in the field of construction. I kept myself open to allowing good to come into my life. I also steered my own opportunities by continually going to school to better myself

The Third Pillar of my belief truly came to fruition when I moved to Oregon and that is TO BLOOM WHEREVER YOU ARE PLANTED. I left a successful job in my home country as an optometrist and then left a good job in San Francisco so I could better provide for my son. While Oregon is not the land of my birth, I have truly flourished here with a successful design career and the creative space and freedom to explore my past, present and future as an artist.

Evelin Marsh

linktr.ee/evelinmarshstudio
PowerfulFemaleImmigrants.com

A LEGACY OF GRATITUDE AND ASPIRATION:

A TRIBUTE TO MY PARENTS AND CHILDREN

Denise Pham, Vietnam

For as long as I can remember, I have always wanted to write a book – but there was a persistent fear that gnawed at me, convincing me I wasn't ready yet. I felt I needed more accolades, achievements, money, and recognition before I could dare to share my stories with the world.

Deep down, I knew my hesitation wasn't just about writing a book; it was about sharing my life experiences and being vulnerable with others. The thought of exposing my struggles and triumphs to the world terrified me. I believed that my story needed to be grand, something extraordinary, to be worthy of telling. But I realized that my journey, though it might not seem grandiose to me, could hold immense power for others. Through small acts of kindness, education, mentoring, and sharing valuable experiences, I can positively influence young and old minds and inspire them to strive for greatness, regardless of their current circumstances or stage in life. If my story can make a positive impact on even one person, then it was all worth it.

In the tapestry of life, I stand, humbled by the profound influence of my parents and the newfound inspiration my children have instilled in me. My journey has been woven with threads of sacrifice, love, and wisdom that I have inherited from my parents, and now, as a parent myself, I am determined to intertwine new threads of progress and growth.

Ah, my dear daughter will probably roll her eyes and never let me forget one of my endearing traits – turning every situation into a life lesson. It's true; I can't help myself. I keep telling her that I wish I had someone like me when I was in my teenage years to share insights that could have saved me years of headaches and heartache. Whether regarding a simple mishap or a profound moment, I find myself offering insights or a nugget of wisdom. But you know what? I wouldn't have it any other way. So, as I share my story, I will share the life lessons I learned from it and hope that it will resonate and make a difference in someone's outlook. Maybe if it comes from someone who didn't think she was big enough to share, it will be less intimidating and more relatable.

I was born in the aftermath of the Vietnam War, when the country was plagued with turmoil and uncertainty. My parents, burdened by the wounds of war and the limitations of a communist regime, made a very tough decision. With hope and faith as their guiding light, they embarked on a risky journey, leaving behind family, friends, and the familiar culture and shores of Vietnam to seek a brighter future for their kids. My family was part of the "boat people," whose stories and statistics you read about in history books. I am always in awe at how strong and brave my parents were. When we escaped Vietnam, my mom was six months pregnant with my baby sister, rocking on the boat until we found refuge in the camps of Hong Kong before resettling in the United States. My dad was in his forties and pretty much had to start from scratch, learning a new language and navigating through unfamiliar territories.

My life lesson: The love my parents had for my siblings and me and their desire to give us a better opportunity in the United States was bigger than their fear of getting caught in Vietnam. If we can change our mindset and focus on what we want to accomplish instead of what is holding us back, we will have a better chance of accomplishing it. Had my parents allowed their fears to hold them back, I would not be sharing this story about how they have inspired me to go for what I want. As a parent, I will continue to encourage my children not to let fear stop them from achieving their dreams.

In high school, I developed a keen interest in golf. My school lacked a girls' golf team, but that didn't deter me. I asked to join the boys' golf team. I ended up secretly dating one of the players on the opposing team, as our parents did not allow us to date until we graduated from college. However, this relationship was short-lived. During a golf game, we were paired together, and as I teed off, my skills impressed his dad, who was there watching. The moment of pride quickly turned into an awkward situation when his dad made a comment about how his son should take golf lessons from me. The embarrassment my "boyfriend" then felt made him uneasy, and the incident pretty much ended the relationship. This was my first time facing the harsh reality of how society sometimes views strong and capable females as a threat to traditional gender roles. It was disheartening to see that my abilities were seen as a challenge to my boyfriend's masculinity instead of a fun competition. This experience made me realize the unfair expectations and prejudices that society imposed on women who dared to stand out and excel.

My life lesson - I will not compromise my performance to appease others' insecurities. However, as an adult reflecting now, I do have compassion for him. I cannot imagine what else his father said to him to make him feel bad. I try to be aware of the things I say to my children in front of their friends because I do not ever want to make my children feel insecure or embarrassed. As a parent, my ultimate desire is to create a loving, understanding, and supportive environment for my children. Nurturing an open relationship with them is essential in helping them feel valued, accepted, and free to express themselves without fear of judgment or disapproval.

Whenever I spend time with my mom, I always reflect on my childhood and the sacrifices she made for our family. She devoted her life to taking care of my father and my siblings. Growing up, my mom would work for 12 hours, six days a week at a Vietnamese restaurant. On her day off, she would go to the grocery to buy food and spend most of her time in the kitchen cooking the most delicious meals ever. That is why I have become such a snob about Vietnamese food. Her dedication has shaped the person I had become, and I feel an overwhelming sense of gratitude for everything she has done for us.

Ironically, I remember during one of our calls, she told me she felt guilty for not being around much when we were kids and not providing us all the extra activities she now sees her grandkids engaging in. I lovingly scolded her for thinking that way and thanked her for her unwavering sacrifices that have molded me into the strong, independent woman I am today. Witnessing her relentless dedication fuels my determination to give my best. Her unconditional love has been the foundation of our family, and her selflessness has shaped us into compassionate and caring individuals. Of course, even when she retired from working at the restaurant, she still spends her time watching her many grandchildren, who also love her cooking.

My life lesson - You know that saying, "I'm turning into my mom?" I couldn't be prouder as I see her strength, love, and resilience reflected in the person I am becoming. While my mom expresses guilt over my childhood, I have guilt as a daughter as she ages. Life has become increasingly busy for me, juggling work, parenting, and the responsibilities that came with adulthood. I am trying to be more intentional with setting my boundaries and making time for my children, mom, family and friends.

My own journey of self-discovery as a parent has allowed me to understand my parents' sacrifices and love on a deeper level. I appreciate the challenges they faced as immigrants in a foreign land, navigating cultural differences and striving to create a better life for their children. Their actions were driven by love, although the methods might have been shaped by cultural norms.

I have come to understand that the greatest gift I could give my children was the freedom to be themselves authentically. I wanted to be a guide and a supporter, allowing them to pursue their passions and make choices based on their interests and abilities.

I found myself consciously avoiding the pitfalls of perpetuating cultural stereotypes. Instead, I chose to celebrate diversity and encourage open-mindedness in my children, teaching them the importance of respecting and valuing every individual's uniqueness. I wanted them to know that their worth was not measured solely by grades but by the content of their character and their impact on the world around them. In breaking free from cultural stereotypes, I hoped to pave the way for my children to embrace their heritage proudly while forging their own paths. As they grew and flourished, I saw how their happiness and confidence radiated from within, and I knew that I was making the right choice by nurturing their individuality.

I cherished every joyful moment with my kids, supporting them through the inevitable trials and tribulations of life. Seeing my son's passion for fishing or my daughter exuding confidence on the basketball court, I am reminded that they are living their lives authentically and unapologetically. As I watch my children grow and thrive, I realize that they are teaching me just as much as I am guiding them. Their passions have become a powerful reminder that breaking free from traditional expectations can lead to genuine happiness and self-fulfillment. For that, I am eternally grateful and profoundly happy.

I found strength in my roots and used my unique experiences to create a powerful narrative for myself and connect with others. My path was not without challenges, but I knew that embracing who I truly was would lead to making remarkable achievements, shattering barriers, and inspiring generations to come.

Testimonials

"Denise is a truly amazing inspiration. Her radiant aura exudes an inherent passion and innate ability to uplift others. This warmth and generosity touches people's lives. She stands strong through adversity and inspires greatness within those around her, especially aspiring women of color. She inspires me to learn and grow by taking chances while empowering others along the journey. Denise is a powerful force for positive change, representing the strength of resilience, drive, and extraordinary kindness." Kat

"Coaching Denise's daughter in basketball has been an absolute joy. Denise's immediate recognition of my potential as a coach and her unwavering support for our business have been incredibly uplifting. Her positive energy and inspiration have made a significant impact, and I am truly grateful to have her as a valued member of our team. She has been a true north star for us." Kenji

"Denise is always such a bright light, and her positivity is always felt by everyone. Denise leads by example and has shown that it is not only okay to ask, but to need help, and that there are still women in this world who are willing to do everything in their power to do so. Her being one of them ." Kalani

"Thank you for all your life lessons and advice this weekend. I'm so touched, and I can't wait to use them to improve my relationship with my parents and partner. You are so incredibly sweet and fun to be around. I'm so glad we met got so much love to go around!!" Lian

---

Denise Pham

Denise Pham is a multifaceted individual whose passion for continuous learning and dedication to various roles in her life have made her an exemplary figure in her community. Born in Vietnam and raised in California, she received her undergraduate degree in Political Science from UC Davis and a Master's in Public Administration from Cal State East Bay.

As an entrepreneur and business consultant, Denise has demonstrated her ability to think strategically and creatively. Her entrepreneurial ventures have allowed her to travel locally and across the nation, promoting growth and innovation.

Denise is also a licensed Realtor®, skillfully guiding clients through the complexities of the real estate market. Her integrity, dedication, and interpersonal skills have earned her a reputation as a trustworthy and reliable real estate professional.

Denise's commitment to empowering others extends beyond the boardroom and into her role as a mentor. She has positively impacted the lives of aspiring young professionals, sharing her knowledge and experiences to inspire the next generation of leaders. She belongs to and is involved in several non-profit projects.

As a devoted parent, Denise takes immense pride in being the #1 cheerleader to her two teenage kids. She actively supports their multiple and ever-changing endeavors, always encouraging them to chase their dreams and embrace their passions.

When she is not doing all the above, she can be found hanging at her anti-gravity yoga class, hiking or walking the trails, volunteering, or finding something adventurous to do.

Connect with her at

DenisePham.com

PowerfulFemaleImmigrants.com

SPELLS OF EMPOWERMENT

TURNING "WHY ME?" INTO "WATCH ME!"

Elise Lin, Taiwan

I am grateful for the opportunity to tell my story. The truth is that I had blocked out most of my childhood memories because of their painful nature. "Why am I here? Why did God bring me into this world to endure suffering? These questions echoed within me from a tender age. Even as a five-year-old child, I grappled to comprehend why I had been brought into this world only to be subjected to torture and abuse. Fear gripped my every waking moment, and I yearned for an escape, a way out of the darkness. Later, in my twenties, I found the courage to embark on a self-discovery journey and inner healing that profoundly impacted every aspect of my life. The rewards I have reaped from this transformation are truly immeasurable. My sincere hope is that my story will inspire others to explore their inner selves and discover their inherent divinity.

I was born in Taipei, Taiwan, with an older sister and a younger brother. Despite being part of the family, I always felt like an outsider. From the beginning, my mother harbored an unexplainable hatred towards me, fueled by my father's infidelities. This hatred manifested as mental, emotional, and physical abuse. Her attacks left permanent imprints on my body with a series of bites on my arm and toes. I still have marks from brutal stabbings of pencils on my wrist, chest, and hands. My ears bled countless times as her nails relentlessly pierced into the delicate auricles of my ears. Whenever I took too long to finish my homework, she would twist a pencil between my fingers until they swelled and blistered. She would thrust my head into the toilet at her whim, releasing her anger upon me whenever the need arose. Her rage knew no bounds. She took whatever object was within her reach—a broom, a hanger, a scissor, even her own teeth—to inflict pain upon me, locking the door to prevent anyone from interfering. I was constantly subjected to her fury while my siblings remained untouched. She told me that I was hers and she could beat me to death if she wanted to. It was a bewildering and tormenting experience, as I cried, not understanding why I was the sole target of such brutal abuse.

My self-esteem suffered, and growing up, I was very shy and timid, petite in size, and usually the smallest person in any room, even to this day. I am 4'11", my sister is 5'6", and my brother is 6'. My relatives believed that being fed only rice contributed to my small stature, while my siblings received nutritious meals. Yes, the abuse even extended to food – or lack thereof. By comparison, my sister was the beautiful swan and I was the ugly duckling. She was treated as a princess, and I was treated like Cinderella. She had lovely braided hair with shiny hair pins, wore fancy dresses and shoes, and even had dimples that pleased our mother. She was very charming. I, on the other hand, felt inadequate, afraid to speak up due to the slaps on the cheeks I would receive. My hair was short, like a boy's, and I wore my sister's hand-me-downs. I felt ugly and invisible.

Washing our family's clothes by hand was part of my responsibilities since we didn't have a washing machine, and I wasn't allowed to go to school until all the laundry was washed and hung. Often, I would be late to school and face the teacher's beating as well. Upon returning home, I had to sweep and scrub the floors on my knees, cook rice, wash vegetables, and prepare dinner while my siblings and cousins played outside. Only after finishing all the chores could I finally do my homework. My mother used to call me a midget and ugly, predicting that no one would want to marry me and that I would end up as someone's maid someday.

My weekend visits to my grandmother's house were a sanctuary from the chaos at home. In her presence, I felt a rare sense of safety and comfort. Her smile enveloped me, her warm embrace provided solace, and the treats she offered were tokens of love. As she gently tended to my bruises and wounds, she assured me that one day, this suffering would end and fade from memory. Her words ignited a flame of hope within me. In my heart, she was my true mother. Time seemed to stand still when I was by her side. The hardest moments were when I had to leave her home, knowing I was returning to my misery. Clinging tightly to her legs, I resisted letting go, desperately longing for the freedom and peace she provided. On the way home, my heart cried out, silently pleading with God to release me from my mother's torment. This plea echoed in my mind like a mantra; I must have uttered it a million times.

Out of desperation, I made two attempts to run away from home at ages eight and ten, but both proved unsuccessful. Each time, I found myself back at the place I longed to escape, enduring even harsher punishment for daring to flee. Thankfully, my uncle, who witnessed the bruises and scars that marred my body, intervened and demanded action from my father, who lived in the United States. Eight days before my thirteenth birthday, not knowing a word of English, I set foot on American soil, commencing a journey that would forever alter the course of my life. Countless prayers and pleas had been answered, and though my body still bore the scars of my past, my heart was brimming with renewed hope.

At the age of 16, I finally moved out of my mother's house. Living on my own, I managed to graduate high school with honors. I even had the privilege of delivering the salutatorian speech, sending a message that resonated with my whole being: "If your mind can conceive it, your heart can believe it, you can achieve it," as expressed by Napoleon Hill. Armed with this mantra, I continued my education, earning a degree in telecommunication management with a perfect 4.0 GPA. Filled with determination, I began my ascent up the corporate ladder, starting as a network technician at T-Mobile and then progressing to roles as a software engineer and network engineer. I was ready to conquer the world.

Fast forward to my twenties. Even though physical abuse was a thing of the past, the emotional and mental scars persisted, casting a shadow over my life. Seeking love and validation, I found myself repetitively caught in destructive relationships. The burden of existence became almost too much to bear, driving me to the brink of suicide. But, miraculously, through divine intervention, a newfound strength surged within me, like a lifeline pulling me through each moment. I could not fathom where this spiritual power came from, but it was enough to keep me going, to propel me forward.

Just as the saying goes, "When the student is ready, the master shows up." It seemed as if the universe conspired in my favor. Books practically fell off the shelves, and invitations to enlightening events and seminars landed at my feet, as if a door had cracked open, beckoning me toward inner transformation. I immersed myself in the wisdom of renowned authors such as Wayne Dyer, Louise Hay, Ernest Holmes, Joseph Murphy, Florence Scovel Shinn, Charles Fillmore, Thich Nhat Hanh, and many others. I began to explore and experiment with various healing modalities, including Reiki, Silva Mind Method, Vipassana meditation, the 12-step program, neural linguistic programming, hypnotherapy, dance therapy, you name it. With each modality, my life began to shift, like a puzzle slowly coming together.

Through the process of self-introspection, a profound inward liberation took place at the very core of my being. I was able to shatter the chains of my past, realizing that I am not defined by the pain I've endured. I am not bound to the limitations that others have imposed on me. This mind-blowing breakthrough led me to be completely honest with myself. I came to see that my outer reality reflected the energy I emanated from within. I began to perceive negative people or circumstances as nothing more than wake-up calls. Instead of blaming others or wallowing in self-pity, I began to take charge and dare myself to contemplate the realm of possibilities that my life could be.

Understanding that change is an inside job that begins with my thoughts, I learned to consciously shift my mindset. I began to envision how I wanted to perceive myself and my life, setting bold and clear intentions to steer my path. Unraveling limiting beliefs was not easy, but I persevered. Seeking wisdom, knowledge, and guidance, I fostered a deep connection with the Divine. With enormous gratitude, I have come to the most profound awakening that life is always for me, not against me. Unbeknownst to me in childhood, my inner Divine Self has been my companion all along. Forgiveness has become a potent force in my healing journey, leading me to make peace with those who have hurt me. The nightmares that once haunted my sleep have given way to serenity and tranquility. Most important of all, I have extended forgiveness and compassion to myself, to the little girl within, acknowledging my worthiness and deservingness of self-love and self-acceptance. Gradually, joy has seeped into my being, and I have found contentment in simply embracing my true self.

With every step on this empowering path, I have journeyed closer to my creator and to the person I am destined to become. By honoring my authentic self and affirming and embodying my divine qualities, I have found the freedom to soar. I am forever grateful for the gift of transformation that has set me on this incredible path of self-empowerment and growth. Each day, I continue to celebrate the magic of my evolution, knowing that the power to manifest my heart's deepest desires lies within me. Healing is an inside job.

My healing journey has given me a strong desire to give back and help others. In 2002, I became a certified IPEC coach. Intrigued by the healing powers of Jesus, between 2001 and 2009, I took all the ministerial courses required for a ministerial degree at the Centers for Spiritual Living founded by Dr. Ernest Holmes. In 2013, I earned my ministerial license from The Seminary of Beloved Community, guided by James Twyman, the creator of the movie *Moses Code*. Today, my life has become a playground of service. Through workshops, online classes, and daily Spiritual Mind Treatments (also known as affirmative prayer), I offer guidance to those in need and help individuals transcend their limiting beliefs and embrace their given inner divinity, so they can create a life that is fulfilling from the inside out.

Today, my heart overflows with gratitude as I reflect upon the blessings that grace my life. I have a beautiful, healthy family, including a loving and supportive husband who shares in my dedication to spiritual growth. We recently celebrated our 20-year anniversary, a testament to the strength of our bond. Together, we are navigating the joys and challenges of parenting two teenagers.

Since 2003, I have been deeply involved in the real estate industry with my husband. We have completed dozens of single-family and mobile home flips, new construction projects, and short-term rentals. We even developed a tree farm in Costa Rica, planting 30,000 trees! For 14 years, we had the pleasure of owning and managing a multifamily apartment complex where the slogan was "Living and Loving It Here!" These endeavors have taught us invaluable lessons about property management, passive income, and creating freedom of time. Presently, we are limited partners in various commercial real estate projects. Through our private equity firm, we have been instrumental in assisting individuals in achieving double-digit returns by offering passive investment opportunities in the multifamily market.

I am forever grateful for the freedom the United States of America granted me. It's a gift that has allowed me to build a life beyond my wildest dreams. While life may throw questions our way about why certain things happen, I've come to realize that knowing why isn't essential. What truly matters is our power to shift from a victim consciousness to a higher state of awareness, and with that shift, we can tap into boundless resources from above. Therefore, every experience, no matter how challenging, can be seen as a valuable gift, guiding us to make positive changes. So, instead of asking, "Why me?" let us boldly declare, "Watch me!" With unwavering confidence, we embrace the journey, knowing that we hold the power to shape our destiny and create a life that aligns with our highest purpose.

I welcome speaking and coaching opportunities. Please feel free to connect with me.

Elise Lin

Elise Lin, a Telecommunication Management graduate with a background in Network Engineering. After dedicating 6 1/2 years to T-Mobile, Elise experienced a profound awakening. She realized that she had been working tirelessly to fulfill someone else's vision. This revelation ignited her entrepreneurial spirit, leading her into the world of transformative coaching.

In her coaching practice, Elise assists individuals in uncovering their core values and shedding limiting beliefs. This deep inner transformation unlocks limitless potential and fosters growth in all aspects of life. It allows them to embrace their true selves, initiate generational healing, and build a lasting legacy while unapologetically living their best lives now.

Elise's journey extends beyond coaching, encompassing multifamily real estate investment ventures. Alongside her husband, a seasoned entrepreneur with a diverse range of experiences, they've ventured into various real estate endeavors including flipping single-family and mobile homes, single family new construction, short term rentals, tree farms, and 31 multifamily units during the past 20 years.

Today, as a managing partner of Multiunit Investing, LLC., Elise serves as a Limited Partner in 608 multifamily real estate units and as a General Partner in a 142-unit multifamily property. Her unwavering mission is to show the world that investing in multifamily properties is a proven pathway to financial wealth. As a multifamily real estate syndicator, her team has created opportunities for individuals to generate passive income through real estate without the headaches of dealing with tenants, termites, or leaking toilets.

Elise's commitment to a life of abundance goes beyond real estate. She passionately shares her coaching expertise, empowering others to lead fulfilling lives and impact humanity positively. Elise firmly believes that 'with God all things are possible'. In her free time, she's a world traveler, a passionate dancer, a seeker of meaningful conversations, a lifelong learner, and a devoted mom.

www.multiunitinvesting.net

PowerfulFemaleImmigrants.com

A GIVERS GAIN

Shelly Ann Miles, Trinidad & Tobago

From Trinidad and Tobago to the USA, here is the journey of a young lady who dared to dream and is making those dreams come true. Fast forward, a proud mom, wife, caregiver, business owner of a successful roofing company and a mortgage company that is set to lend billions within a few years on commercial (multifamily) real estate lending. I proudly show up every day to help others. Now let me bring you back in time to share with you on how the journey began.

Coming to America

On June 7, 1998, my parents' sister and I left everything behind and headed for the United States. I have always dreamed of coming to America! I was only 15 years old when we left the only life, I ever knew for a new one. The sadness didn't hit me until I sat on the plane that I was leaving everything I knew all behind.

Hello, my name is Shelly Miles, and I am a commercial mortgage broker. I am also a mom, a wife, a caregiver to my mother, and co-operator of a roofing company which I run with my husband Jerry Miles. I grew up in the Caribbean Island of Trinidad and Tobago in the small village of Bamboo Settlement #3. I didn't realize it until I was a bit older that my parents, both in their 50's at the time sacrificed everything so that we can have a better life here in the US. My parents had an arranged marriage, and my dad couldn't read or write. They have five daughters! Yes, I said five daughters and I am the youngest. Even though I grew up with no running water in the house and an outhouse I thought we were one of the wealthiest families in our village because my parents created a safe space for us. I can honestly say I've had the best childhood memories a girl can ask for.

I moved to Kentucky about four weeks later after we landed in the US. I was away from my parents for the first time in 15 years, because I had to start school. My parents who stayed in Virginia to work would join me in 6 months. I lived with one of my aunts in Kentucky who was helping us get our new lives started. She enrolled me in a small private Christian school. It was different, as I was different from all the kids. I was darker and I didn't speak proper English. No, I don't speak another language, we spoke English with a dialect, we speak really fast and it's difficult to understand at times. I made friends right away. Everyone was friendly and treated me kindly even though I felt, sound, and look different. They were curious and I enjoyed their curiosity. My husband Jerry and I met on one of the first days I started high school and no, we weren't high school sweethearts, but we have always liked each other. He was the star of the high school basketball team and I was his assigned cheerleader. We started dating in 2001 right after I graduated from high school and we got married June of 2005.

Pregnancy Scare

When I got pregnant with my first baby JJ, I was working full-time as an assistant manager at the mall, and we bought our first home. During the end of my second trimester, I started having contractions. My doctor put me on strict bedrest. I had to leave my job and I was scared because it was my first pregnancy. Our family and friends from church came together and made sure we were taken care of with meals. We felt the love and the presence of God. JJ was born on March 12, 2006. Even though he was early he was the healthiest baby boy. I was a proud mama and the joy I had was indescribable.

My pregnancy scare got us much closer to God. Maybe the Lord spoke to us at the same time I'm not sure, but we made a commitment to start tithing at church. We had a healthy baby boy, and Jerry had a great job with a construction company. Even though the construction job took him out of town and me being at home alone with a new baby the money was great. On that next Thanksgiving holiday Jerry came home with one of the biggest paychecks he had ever received. He intended on heading back out to work after that weekend. We decided to use the money to pay off the bills and told ourselves we would pay our tithes on the next paycheck. Unfortunately, the construction company lost a big contract and went under before they could head back out. Jerry never worked for them again. For me, that was a sign, because I didn't feel right about not tithing. When God speaks, we should listen. With both of us not working, we were at a crossroad. Jerry and his dad were experienced in roofing, so they started a roofing company, and I jumped in to help with payroll.

Unexpected Pain

On January 13, 2007, I was at the mall with my mom after I picked her up from work. My dad worked as a janitor at the mall. We were having dinner in the cafeteria thinking my dad was at home because he would leave work around 3 o'clock. One of his coworkers came up to us and said, "is everything OK?" but we didn't know what she was talking about. She then proceeded to tell us that an ambulance came and took my dad to the hospital. My mom had just gotten off work at 5pm and didn't check her voicemail. We jumped in the car and headed straight to the hospital, my immediate thoughts were he's hurt, and he's probably upset because we were taking so long to come to the hospital. When we arrived, my sister was already there, and all I can remember was seeing her and her husband walking out through double doors from a hallway, and she was crying, but I was confused because I never thought the worst could happen. There was a guy that ushered us into a room nearby and my sister was just bawling her eyes out, I kept asking her what? what? what is it? I was thinking my dad got hurt at work and it was really bad, but I never ever thought what I was about to hear. She said "he's gone!! Daddy is gone." My dad was no longer here, and I immediately felt numb. I've never felt this way before, I was dizzy it felt like I was in a dream a nightmare. I have never experienced anyone so close to me dying. My dad was the best dad. I have only great memories of him. He was caring and so funny I wish my kids had gotten to know him. I see so much of him in them, and it brings me joy. My sisters and I do keep his memories alive by telling the kids stories about him.

He was found at work in a stair well sitting. He had a heart attack and passed away; I would like to think he fell asleep. We had no money for a funeral, and he had no life insurance. Again, family and friends came together to help with what they could, and our church stepped in to helped with the rest. It was a blessing!

Our Real Estate Journey

Starting a new business was hard. Jerry and I didn't go to college and had no business background. We were struggling to make ends meet and lost our 1st home. We relied on his dad's business experience. All of this was happening during the 2006 to 2008 market crash. The roofing business started to do well, and we moved into a new home which we rented at 1st and then purchased. I started getting more involved in the roofing business and we eventually took it over from his father. We never forgot the Lord in all that had happened and continue to faithfully tithe. I did the administrative part and was a stay-at-home mom and unfortunately, my mom who has lived with us since my dad died was diagnosed with dementia in 2018, and I became her caregiver. We have decided to keep my mom close us and God by having her live in our home.

She is part of the reason why we are here in America. In our culture we take care of our elders and we have chosen to keep our tradition alive, the Bible says, "Honor your father and mother." It's the only commandment with a promise.

Jerry has always had a love for real estate and eventually I grew to love it as well. Almost 8 years ago, we bought our first rehab. It was a duplex, and it didn't need much work. We painted it, replace some doors, did tiles in the bathroom, and installed new gutters. We had no trouble renting it out. We paid cash for it, so it was free and clear.

We decided to refinance it and buy another one so we can do the same. Since we were self-employed, our plan was to buy at least two houses a year and rent them out. This was going to support our retirement plans. But little did we know that by being self- employed the local banks looked at us differently. We tried for a while and couldn't get a loan. Eventually Jerry started calling hard money lenders. Some of them thought we were silly for asking for a loan that was under $100,000. Finally, we got someone to say OK but... There was a catch! The broker wanted an extra $10,000 on top of his fee he was already receiving. It really wasn't worth it, and we felt taken advantage of. We ended up not doing the deal. The situation got him doing some research on the commercial lending world. He came across the school that trained you on how to be a broker for all businesses. He saw a need for someone to bring these products to the market in a fair and honest way. Because I was living comfortably it took him about two years to convince me we needed something like this. I finally said yes! The school allowed for two people to go to Albany, New York for seven days of training. But with two young kids, a mother with dementia and a roofing company it was a challenge.

They allowed us to come separately so Jerry went first in September 2019 while I took care of things at home, and I went in October 2019. Even though I was out of my comfort zone, traveling by myself, and leaving my babies for so long. I am glad I did because of that; *Adventure Commercial Capital* was born. "Only those who risk going too far can possibly find out how far they can go."

New Beginnings to Financial Freedom

The training was a crash course with a lifetime access to any of the classes, teachers and lenders. We both graduated. We were set and ready to work. We did some cold calling, some door-to-door knocking, and even did an email blast to let everyone know that we were in business. At the beginning of 2020 we did Google Ads Marketing. We had about eight loans in the pipeline. Unfortunately, as you all know in March 2020 Covid hit and the whole country shut down. Lenders halted all lending. We got cold feet and we shut everything down with the hopes of opening back up eventually. We decided to go bigger and started tithing not just on the profits but on our gross income. The Lord was pouring his blessings on us. Our roofing business got busier than ever, and we signed our biggest paying job during that time. We assume the Lord was leading us in that direction. In April 2022 we started this big job. The paperwork ended up being tedious. It was a prevailing wage job which means it was a government regulated paying job. It was a nightmare! Anyways, I had had enough! and we still had dreams of making the lending business work. We knew it was going to take some time and hard work, but we didn't know how to scale our new business in these trying times.

All in God's Timing

JJ, my oldest when he was probably about 13 or 14 years old a very ambitious kid by the way, he would always talk about some guy that wrote a book called the 10X something, where you can 10X your goals. Yes! You guessed it, it's Grant Cardone with the 10X Rulebook. I never really paid attention to JJ except for when he would come to me and say, "Mom! this guy said you don't have to go to college to create wealth." As a mom, all I heard was this guy was telling my kids not to go to school. So, I will tell him to stop listening to him. But him and Jerry would keep talking about Grant.

So, in May 2022, I was searching I didn't know what I was searching for. We had put a lot of money into our commercial lending business, and it was just sitting there. I prayed and a fire was lit under me to do something. One day I was scrolling through Facebook and Grant Cardone popped up on my feed with one of his ads. He was doing a free four-hour business workshop on a Saturday, so I blindly signed up for it. I felt like I had nothing to lose, and it was free. And guess what? I made JJ and Jerry sit with me during that class. I started to realize that this guy is very cocky, but he made a lot of sense. Anyways, after the workshop we signed up for a three-day 10X VIP Business Boot Camp. It was such an awesome event! It was what we were looking for to take our business to the next level. One thing led to the next, and we ended up in Grant Cardone's real estate club. This puts us in front of some big real estate investors. One of my favorite quotes is "Do not wait for opportunities, create it." -George Bernard Shaw.

Grant always says, "You need to be in the right room." And this puts us in the right room. So here we are, all in God's timing. Every day we are pushing and focusing on helping others with their real estate journey!

"You will get all you want in life, if you help enough
other people get what they want,"
-Zig Ziglar

Shelly Miles

Migrated from the small Caribbean Island of Trinidad & Tobago to the USA when I was 15 years old. With no college education I am a proud business owner of a successful Commercial Roofing Company & A Commercial Mortgage Broker & Cofounder of *Adventure Commercial Capital* that is set to lend billions over the next couple of years. I am a

Proud mom to 2 handsome young men JJ 17 & Jordan 14, a wife, and caregiver to my mom. I have a love for real estate and have bought and sold a few with my husband. I love doing the interior designs on our properties and telling my husband what to do, lol.

I want to help others in their real estate journey. My focus is to match you with the right lender. Each property is unique, and each buyer is unique. Because we have had difficulty finding the right lender for us, we have started *Adventure Commercial Capital.* We host a free bi-weekly educational commercial mortgage Debt Financing Zoom class every other week, for more information you can reach me at www.adventurecomcap.com We co-host with The Multifamily Freedom Chasers community in helping educate others on real estate investing..

Why am I doing this? You might ask. I'm doing this for my kids, my husband, my mom, for financial freedom, to help my church with the many ministries they have. I want to bring as many people with me as I can on this journey. And I want to travel the world! "When you feel like quitting, think about why you started."

I don't know where I would be today if it wasn't for my Lord and Savior, Jesus Christ, and for my husband the love of my life for pushing me to be the woman I am today!

I also love being on the water with my family, playing volleyball, decorating cakes, taking pictures of nature and I love America!

Here's how to reach me.

shelly@adventurecomcap.com

PowerfulFemaleImmigrants.com

FIGHT, FLY AND FREEDOM
A TALE OF STRUGGLE, SELF DISCOVERY AND PURPOSE

Mary Cardenas, Philippines

Fight, Fly, and Freedom are stages of personal growth that can guide you, help you understand your current situation, and navigate you towards rising above challenges.

"Fight" denotes a phase in which you encounter obstacles or resistance. It entails recognizing and confronting your struggles, using this awareness as a catalyst for personal growth.

"Fly" signifies a stage where you leverage your natural abilities or resources to overcome challenges. It's about harnessing what is innately available to you, moving forward by trusting in your abilities and skills.

"Freedom" reflects the stage where you transcend your circumstances and utilizing it to evolve into a state of liberation. It signifies the ability to not be defined by your situation, but to use it as a stepping stone to achieve more and realize your true potential.

When combined, these stages can provide one with the insight needed to understand their current position in life. Moreover, this can serve as a mechanism to illuminate the path to overcome your obstacles and lead the way to achieve greater heights.

As a child, I was not acquainted with these concepts, but as I matured and sought greater understanding, I began to gain awareness of my personal struggles through the recognition of the aspects of my identity. Naturally, as we journey through life, we will all encounter fresh challenges and conflicts, uncover new aspects of our identity, and strive to transcend these situations. I believe that you can utilize the concepts of fight, fly, and freedom as a compass to navigate the complexities of our shared human experience.

I invite you to immerse yourself in my narrative and discover your own reflections within it. Journey with me from the struggles I have encountered at various life stages, through my self-discovery, comprehension of my true self, and to the point where I am now -drawing ever closer to the level where I sense that freedom is within grasp.

Act 1: Humble Beginnings

As a child in the province of the Philippines, my days started very early. At 4 am on a Saturday, while it was still dark outside and the air felt cool on my skin, my mom would quietly tell me to wake up so we could gather our vegetables and sell them at the market. After a few hours of picking up vegetables and cleaning them, I would then go with my dad to the farmers market. As a young kid selling produce in a busy market, I had to speak in a loud manner so people would notice me. On the marketing side, I knew that by organizing the tomatoes neatly, made it easier for buyers to pick and led to more sales.

On a good day, I made the equivalent of $5. After selling the vegetables, I would buy a pound of fish or meat from the market. The process of bringing home meat was exciting for my family because it was a change from only eating the vegetables from our garden. While we were not starving, we had to be careful with our portions to feel full. Despite the challenges, we stayed strong and learned important lessons about hard work and resourcefulness.

Within the walls of our home, we found happiness and joy. But once outside, comparing our possessions with others who seemed to have more material things, I could not help but doubt our situation in life. As I grew older, those who seemed to have more opportunities and possessions got harder to simply ignore. Envy took root in my heart, and I questioned my own self worth and capabilities. I began to believe that good things in life were only for the rich and "deserving" individuals.

Working diligently to assist my family was my inherent *'fly'* stage. The hustle of selling vegetables to ensure that we had food on our table, or aiding with household tasks like traveling on foot to fetch clean water, was second nature. It was indeed hard work, but it did not wear me out because it was fueled by my desire to care for my family. The phase of *'fight'* and struggle surfaced when I began comparing my circumstances with others. The struggle was intense because I failed to appreciate the value and beauty inherent in my own situation - we were together and that is what should have mattered most.

Gradually, I began to understand that true flourishing resided not in external circumstances but within my own being. I discovered that no matter what life threw at me, I had the essential qualities needed to overcome adversity. This newfound belief transformed my perspective and gave me the strength to face the many challenges in life. It was at this pivotal moment that I uncovered an inspiring sense of *freedom* from my circumstances. My situation no longer held any sway, as it merely became a catalyst for the rich tapestry of life lessons - a testament to love, resilience, and a profound understanding that these experiences had instilled in me.

Act 2: Discovering My Authentic Self

In the middle of the school year in 1995, when I was fifteen years old, my family received exciting yet bittersweet news – we were moving to Canada to start a new life. As a teenager, I was just beginning to discover myself and gain confidence at school. I felt like I had the potential to thrive, and I formed a close group of friends who became like family to me. I had achieved the status of being popular, a top student, and someone everyone wanted to hang out with.

Everything shifted when we relocated to Canada. With my pronounced accent and second-hand clothes that made me look like a 15-year-old dressing as a 50-year-old woman, I felt out of place. Since English was my second language, articulating my thoughts was a struggle. I felt a disconnect with the other kids who had grown up there. Self-doubt started to creep in and I began to retreat into my shell. As my struggles persisted, I gradually began to fight for clarity and understanding. I made a conscious decision to embrace my uniqueness. It was a slow process, but eventually, I learned to appreciate my accent and all the aspects that shaped my identity. This newfound self-acceptance and love launched me on a journey of self-discovery, empowerment, and freedom. I found liberation from doubting my capabilities and feeling inadequate. I realized I was worthy and capable.

In my early years, I had a strong desire to become a business owner and entrepreneur. During playtime, I loved teaching younger kids, selling products, and interacting with my peers about our merchandise. This dream held a special place in my heart throughout my childhood. However, as I grew into my teenage and adult years, I started to lose sight of the possibilities.

As high school graduation approached, I realized that I had to make some choices. I understood that completing my education was vital for a better future. However, I knew I had much to discover about myself and the courage needed to dive deep within.

Presented with the choice between Business School and Computer Science, my initial inclination was towards business. But, having strayed from my childhood dream of becoming an entrepreneur, I found the challenge of Computer Science alluring. I opted for this field and it gradually morphed into my new identity. After graduation, I relished the role of a Quality Engineer in the Technology Industry. The essence of uniting engineers towards shared goals and experiencing the camaraderie among them as they built something together inspired me to give my all to the field of Engineering.

Sometimes in life, we end up choosing paths that diverge vastly from our dreams. As we struggle and fight to navigate these paths, they start to feel natural. We begin to adapt them into our daily existence, and soon enough, they become our new identity.

My journey into family life was not easy, but now things are going well. It took dedication, hard work, perseverance, and unwavering faith to create the beautiful family life I have today.

I moved to Californian right out of college. The shift felt like I started all my life all over over again. I had no family but made new friends in the community.

Two years later, I found myself pregnant outside of marriage. I knew it wouldn't be easy, but I was ready to face the challenges that lay ahead. Being a mom felt natural to me, but the flood of emotions, uncertainty, and fear overwhelmed me, leaving me feeling lost and alone. The thought of having my son without the support of a partner was one of the toughest fight I've ever faced. Each night, tears soaked my pillow as I grappled with the gravity of this life-changing situation. However, in that vulnerable moment, I discovered a wellspring of courage within me. With profound faith and the unwavering support of my partner, family, and close friends, I bravely chose to embrace life fully and welcome the birth of my child. This experience filled me with an unbreakable thread of love and resilience, illuminating a new path ahead with newfound purpose and determination. Through hard work and continuous faith, the father of my son, who is now my husband, and I live peaceful and share beautiful lives together with our three children.

My journey through high school, college, and adult years was strewn with struggles. Every stage presented its unique challenges - from grappling with insecurities during high school, enduring periods when I lacked faith in myself, to confronting the sting of loneliness. Amidst these struggles, my aim was to delve deeper into understanding myself. To unearth what was authentically me and to explore what it would mean to 'fly' in the face of these tribulations, leveraging my natural instincts. To hearken to the voice within me rather than the echoes of self-doubt. The act of transcending these challenges involved a return to self-love and acceptance. Recognizing that our inherent state is one of love, represents the essence of freedom - a freedom that is ours to claim and relish.

Through all this, I learned a valuable lesson that I want to share with you: Embrace your uniqueness and be proud of who you are. Life may throw unexpected challenges your way, but when you stay true to yourself, you unlock the power within to overcome anything.

Always bear in mind that the power of resilience and love can unlock your freedom to grow and find fulfillment. Greet every phase of your life with an open heart and relentless resolve, because you have the capability to craft a beautiful and inspiring narrative that is uniquely yours.

Act 3: Purpose Beyond Self

Throughout my life, I have faced and overcome various challenges. Little did I know that these obstacles were preparing me for my true calling - to give wholeheartedly and be a servant to others. This calling led me to venture into real estate, not just for financial gain, but with a greater purpose - to positively impact causes dear to my heart and uplift those who supported me.

As a real estate investor, I was driven to impart my wisdom and experiences, particularly to those striving for financial stability in their future. My goal was to enable individuals to carve out their definition of freedom and devise strategies to alter their present circumstances, thereby realizing their aspirations.

I became an advocate for informed decision-making, particularly in the multifamily market, where stable returns and long-term growth potential existed. I felt a deep responsibility to break down complex concepts, demystify potential risks, and highlight the abundant investment opportunities available.

Beyond sharing information, I aimed to foster lasting, positive relationships between investors and property owners or management companies. Trust and mutual understanding were crucial to successful partnerships in real estate, and I made it a priority to facilitate connections and create an environment where all parties could thrive.

This journey of educating and uplifting others became a cornerstone of my life's work, bringing a profound sense of fulfillment and purpose. It solidified my belief that we can shape a better, more inclusive world where opportunities abound for everyone. Together with a united community, we embarked on a mission to support, encourage, and empower one another, weaving a profound difference in the lives of others through boundless giving.

My personal narrative is a testament to the power of the fight, the liberation in the flight, and the beauty in the freedom. This tale of resilience, self-discovery, and altruism stands as a beacon of hope in the face of life's adversities. Through faith in oneself, in others, and in the boundless potential the future holds, we collectively strive for a more compassionate world.

Let my journey serve as a reminder that life's unexpected twists and turns can lead us to discover our true purpose. Embrace the humility of your beginnings, uncover your genuine self, and seek out a calling that extends beyond you. Keep your dreams close, even when they seem unattainable, as they might hold the key to your ultimate satisfaction.

Claim your freedom by staying authentic to who you are and acknowledge that your aspirations and dreams are attainable. It comes with a profound understanding of our inherent state of being. Flying is essentially embodying our true selves. It's about embracing our distinct qualities and uniqueness. Trust in the extraordinary magic that resides within you, guiding you towards infinite possibilities and self-transformation. Embrace your journey and your purpose, and let it serve as a lighthouse of hope and inspiration for others to follow.

May you continue to fly, harness your innate abilities, and obtain resources needed to overcome challenges. Trust in your skills and keep propelling forward. May you find liberation by rising above your circumstances to reach a state of freedom. This one is to discovering your true potential. May God's blessings be with you on this journey.

Mary Cardenas

In 2022, Mary Cardenas took a leap into the real estate world, with a keen interest in multi-family properties. She founded BILAJ Capital Partners with a mission to educate and foster a community of investors. Through this platform, she aimed to equip her investors with the necessary tools to smartly leverage their hard-earned money and venture boldly into fruitful real estate opportunities. With an unwavering focus and an eye for detail, she consistently stays ahead of the curve. Every investment she undertakes is meticulously planned, ensuring that it's not just profitable for her, but also advantageous for everyone involved. Her proactive approach and commitment make her stand out and build trust among her partners and investors.

Before stepping into real estate, Mary had a strong tech background. As a Staff Quality Engineer in the San Francisco Bay Area, she worked with several top tech firms. Mary has a Computer Science degree from the University of Manitoba in Canada. With her solid education and practical experience, she built a strong foundation that later helped her thrive in real estate.

Outside work Mary is out embracing life's many adventures. Whether she's tackling a challenging hike, exploring a new corner of the world, or enjoying a delicious new dish in the Bay Area, Mary's all about living life to the fullest. And the best part? She gets to share these special moments with her husband, daughter, and two sons. Together, they make each adventure a cherished memory. Her love for both her career and her hobbies shows that Mary really knows how to blend hard work with a healthy dose of fun!

bilajcapital.com

PowerfulFemaleImmigrants.com

NO MORE EXCUSES, PLEASE – STOP WAITING AND START DOING

WHY YOU CANNOT FAIL WHEN YOU STAY IN ACTION MODE

Barbara Heil-Sonneck, Germany

As I sit here, starting to think about the title and headline, I admit that this story is a letter to myself first and foremost. You might think that sounds odd but give me a moment to explain. I am turning 60 soon, and even though I feel like I am 45, sometimes, I am struck by the awakening that time is precious and limited. So, how I invest my time and with whom has become particularly important in planning my day.

At the beginning and ending of each day, I ask myself: Why am I doing this? Will it support my vision? Will it provide value? Will it move someone, or my vision, forward?

Yes, we want to make this world a better place by supporting, helping, and driving change. But how can we do that if we continue to struggle?

There are a ton of shiny objects out there. Specifically, social media provides an everyday picture and a constant flow of interruption if we allow that to happen. So, what do we do to stay focused instead of distracted?

My number one goal is to stop getting sidetracked. Can you relate?

Stay and be the independent individual, don't throw your power away and get lost in being defined by others. Be your own freedom chaser, always and forever.

In *Powerful Female Immigrants Volume 2*, I shared that both the origin of both my parents' families trace back to the "Sudetenland" in former Czechoslovakia, which now encompasses the Czech Republic and Slovakia following their peaceful separation in 1993. Both families had left that area and settled in Germany after World War II. I was raised to be dependable, honest, and respectful of my parents, as well as to obtain a good education, get a job, work hard, not raise my voice, and fit in. This younger me still exists in my head, but boy, has my mindset and my voice changed over time.

Stop trying to be perfect and leap into action. Unleash the power in you!

In this world full of abundant opportunities, it is easy to get caught up in the paradox of choice. We often find ourselves waiting for the "right" moment, the "perfect" opportunity, or the "ideal" circumstances to act. However, this waiting game can become a trap, leading to stagnation and missed opportunities. One pivotal turn in my early life came from starting to go after what I wanted and ask for opportunities. When I later did more research, I found some helpful explanations I wanted to share with you:

The Illusion of Perfection

- Perfection is a myth: No situation or moment will ever be perfect and waiting for perfection can lead to inaction.
- The cost of lost opportunity: While we are waiting for the perfect moment, we are missing out. Time is a resource we never can get back.
- Growth comes from imperfection: Mistakes and failures are inevitable, but they also provide valuable learning experiences.

Trust me, there have been several lessons learned in my life, from wrong job choices to wrong partners, a divorce, a failed project, and a failed venture. However, I always looked at these as opportunities as valuable insight into what not to do again, and without these experiences, I believe I would not be who and where I am today.

The Trap of Comfort Zones

- Fear: Staying put can feel safe, but it prevents us from experiencing new things.
- Stagnation: Without challenges, there is no growth. Staying in our comfort zones can lead to stagnation.
- Taking risks and stepping out of our comfort zones is necessary for personal and professional growth.

The Power of Action

- Learn by doing: The best way to learn is by doing. Action leads to experience, which leads to knowledge and wisdom.
- Momentum: Once you start acting, it's easier to keep going. Momentum can be a powerful motivator.

- Control: By acting, we are taking control of our lives. We are not just reacting to circumstances, but actively shaping our own path.

I genuinely believe in the power of action. When the opportunity was presented to me to leave my home country and accept a position in the United States, I only had one week to decide whether to leave my family, friends, home, and country to venture into the abyss of the unknown. I had met my new boss only once and did not have any other connections or personal contacts in the U.S. I said yes, and the rest is history.

In summary, waiting for the perfect moment or staying within our comfort zones can hold us back from reaching our full potential. It is important to recognize these traps and take proactive steps to overcome them. Remember, the best time to start is now. So, stop waiting, and start doing.

Stop giving up your independence. Never lose *you.*

I consider independence as the ability to make our own decisions in life. It is important to note that it does *not* mean to be alone or only do things our own way, but rather to be liberated from dependence on someone else for our happiness, freedom, and satisfaction.

Independence: Words of Wisdom

We all have the capability to face challenges, make decisions, and take risks. Independence teaches us to rely on ourselves and trust our abilities and judgment. Being independent encourages us to learn new skills and acquire knowledge.

Losing independence can lead to dependency on others, which can make you feel trapped. When we depend on others, we lose control over our lives, as our decisions and actions are influenced by others. Dependency can erode our self-confidence and cause us to start doubting our abilities and decisions.

Why is independence so important to me?

My mom died of cancer when I was 12. My dad was lost, devastated, and he started to drink more than was good for him. I found it was better to stay away from him. Two years later, Dad met a wonderful woman, who had two kids, and we became a patchwork family. My new mom was a blessing, and I suddenly gained an older sister and younger brother. Life started to look sunny again.

I left home when I turned 18. The last year had been quite a struggle. My dad's alcohol intake had increased. We learned to tiptoe around the house to keep the peace. There were good days and bad days. When I left, I walked straight into a psychologically and financially abusive relationship with a man twice my age. At first, I did not even recognize the abuse. At first, I viewed him as highly intelligent and caring – but step by step, I became ensnared in the web of his intrigues and schemes.

After a year and a half, I finally was strong enough to leave in the middle of the night with only the clothes on my back. I knew that I had a long legal fight ahead, since I had co-signed some business papers as part-owner of his company. There I was, 19 years old, in huge debt but with a fresh start. That experience taught me a lot about the legal process and negotiation.

Maintain your Independence - How to never give it up

- Make your own decisions: Always take charge of your life. Bear the consequences; this will help you learn and grow – I live and breathe this.
- Learn new skills: Keep learning new skills. This will not only make you more capable but also more confident. For me, I continue being a student and try something new every year.
- Be financially independent: Strive to earn your own living.
- Build healthy relationships: It is crucial and necessary to have healthy relationships. Just ensure that these relationships do not compromise your independence.

I believe independence is a valuable trait that should never be given up. I guard it fiercely and never let it go. I feel truly blessed in my 22-year relationship with my Mr. Right, a partnership in which we always kept our promise of commitment and independence. The other connections, friendships, and relationships I have built over the years have changed, and so have I. The last two years in have driven a new urgency of aligning on value. My motto is: "Only connect with people who raise your vibration." As such, value alignment is a key component in all relationships. Choose your partners wisely.

Since my childhood, I have always looked at the glass as half full and never let negative thoughts and energy derail me. I have made plenty of mistakes on my journey; however, they all have been stepping stones that have helped me better myself a little bit more every day.

Everything is possible.

I love what I do, and I always look for ways to grow. If you love something, you will find and make time for it. Through my experiences, I have learned how to find opportunities that give me financial independence and long-term stability.

Investing in myself, being a constant student, and having a business and life coach to hold me accountable for my actions have been key to advancing and moving forward. Being extremely specific and selective on value alignment, I surround myself with people who are striving and propelling forward. This is inspiring and drives me to give my absolute best!

In every situation we encounter in our lives, we choose how we perceive and react to it. There is always something to learn from every challenge. Our mind is an amazing vehicle. Dolly Parton once said, "If your actions create a legacy that inspires others to dream more, learn more, do more, and become more, then you are an excellent leader." This is my quote of the year.

So, what is my next step? Besides growing my real estate investment portfolio and collaborating with experienced syndicators, I will continue to speak on podcasts and at conferences as well as start goal-aligned small masterminds. Accountability in a small group setting is a superpower, which has helped me propel forward. I like to extend this opportunity to a selected group of like-minded female entreprenistas. This is my next best secret on the power of collaboration.

If my story inspired you to action, I would love to learn more about you and your goals during a Zoom coffee chat.

Barbara Heil-Sonneck

Barbara Heil-Sonneck is a serial entrepreneur, a savvy real estate investor, and an award-winning designer with a love for travel.

Her mission revolves around helping women leverage their experience and success by harnessing the power of investments and partnerships. Breaking free with diverse income streams, they can move beyond the standard limitations of entrepreneurship or professional careers and design their "rich life" with more passive income while having a massive impact.

She believes in "Atomic Habits" and the "Power of One More" and that aligning with the right partners, assembling the right teams, and honoring core values are key. A trailblazer in many ways, she is not afraid to be uncomfortable, believing that with discomfort comes growth.

Barbara loves to mastermind, sharing her learning and best practices as a business owner. Her viewpoints on heart-centered leadership with authenticity, the power of energy alignment, business growth strategies, shareholder mindset, and team delegation make her a valuable resource for media and those hosting events, podcasts, and expert panels.

Barbara is deeply enthusiastic about legacy building and social impact. Her calling is raising awareness about the fight against human trafficking and collaborating for solutions.

"Be fearless, inspired, unstoppable for change."

The charity of her choice is SAPREA, which has a mission to liberate individuals and society from child sexual abuse and its lasting impacts.

Let's be social and connect:

linktr.ee/barbarahs

PowerfulFemaleImmigrants.com

THE UNSTOPPABLE SUSAN

Susan Noh, Korea

"Susan, can you quickly gather your violin and come with me?"

My Sunday mornings during my high school years in America always kicked off with playing the violin in the church's orchestra. That particular day was no exception to this routine. We had our rehearsal, and everything seemed set for the worship service to begin. But then, one of the church deacons approached me with a trembling voice, urging me to pack up and follow him. His attempt to remain calm was evident.

"Everything will be okay. Your mom called and said your dad has been taken to the emergency room. I'm going to drive you there right away. Let's get moving, but remember, everything will be alright."

Having arrived in the country just a year ago, as a 17-year-old, I didn't fully grasp the implications of someone being admitted to the emergency room. All I knew was that my dad had been experiencing severe pain in his back and had even mentioned partial loss of vision in his right eye. As I gazed out of the moving car, a sense of foreboding washed over me. Somehow, I felt that the peaceful scenery passing by the car window might be the last tranquility I would experience.

Things took a rapid turn for the worse. In January of 2012, my 43-year-old father was hospitalized for what was initially thought to be a widespread infection. He was placed in an isolation room, and our entire family - my mom, myself, and my 8-year-old sister Rachel followed him into the isolation room to stay with him. We were inseparable. Every staff member who visited followed him into the isolation room, was puzzled about our presence there. Nevertheless, there was no way we would leave him alone. This marked the beginning of our arduous yet brief journey of battling my father's stage 4 stomach cancer.

From that point on, all of my father's responsibilities fell directly on my shoulders. I took care of bills, dropped off my sister to school and her extracurricular activities, attended parent-teacher conferences, virtually lived at the hospital as a translator, and provided unwavering support to my family in a country where I was still struggling to understand what was considered normal. In fact, back in Korea, I had only known how to take care of myself as a high school girl, so the transition was overwhelming.

Throughout my father's hospitalization, there were many challenging moments. Not only did I struggle to comprehend the norms, but I often found it difficult to interpret the news shared by doctors and nurses. I had no idea what to say to my dad when his main doctor informed me that he had "*adenocarcinoma*." Unlike in Korea, they didn't provide us with a prognosis for how long he had to live. Every day was a battle, but I never thought that he would actually pass away.

One night, while sleeping in the waiting area of the Intensive Care Unit, my mom urgently called me into the room. At that time, my dad had a pressurized breathing machine due to a collapsing lung caused by fluid buildup, but he was not sedated. When I rushed to his side, I could see that he was trying to leave the room to search for me. He was hungry and struggling for oxygen, not in his right state of mind. I pressed my head against his, and he seemed to calm down as if he had been searching for me all along. Shortly after, an intern informed me that he needed to be intubated, and I requested to speak with an on-call doctor to understand what this meant for my dad. I will never forget the irritated tone of that on-call doctor when I called at 3 a.m.: *"Your father is going to die anyway."*

As much as I hated to admit it, that callous doctor was right. About a month later, the hospital asked us to disconnect the intubation because my dad wasn't improving, and the daily cost of keeping him alive was a significant burden for them.

I thought to myself, *"This decision that I have to make will haunt me forever. It's like ending my own father's life, cutting off his oxygen."*

When my dad passed away in August of the same year, I was at a loss for how to process it. He was young, and I was too. I had never imagined life without him. He was my best friend. There were moments when I woke up in the morning, momentarily forgetting that he was no longer there, and instinctively reached for my phone to call him. I was trying to tell him about my dream. The confusion would set in for the first few minutes, as I couldn't find his number. But when I fully awoke and realized he is no longer here I felt myself plummeting into a deep, spiraling dark sadness.

Yet, I had my family to take care of—my young sister and my non-English-speaking mom. When I started college the following year, there was a period when I maintained full-time student status while working at five different jobs. It was during this time that I met Andre, my life partner, at a real estate office. Back then, I had never even considered dating someone who wasn't Korean. Culturally, it seemed unthinkable, and I doubted I could express my true feelings in a language that wasn't my mother tongue. My mom, naturally, believed I was just being a rebellious young girl by dating someone from Colombia.

Andre understood that I was in dire situation. My mom and I had chosen to live in a costly area to ensure Rachel attended a good school, and we had already been evicted from our previous residence that my dad had rented before falling ill. One day, Andre asked me to jot down ten ways I could make money. One of the options I listed was selling my body parts, such as a kidney. That's how desperate I felt for money. It was a profound lesson in life, teaching me what it's like to have no financial support or safety net.

But who would have guessed that a cheerful, easygoing guy from Colombia, who had also arrived in the country at 16, would cross paths with a serious and determined girl from Korea? We not only became life partners but also embarked on building a successful business empire together.

Our journey into the world of real estate was an unexpected twist, a turn in the story of my life that no one could have foreseen during those dark days in the hospital. It was a testament to resilience, a response to desperation that transformed into determination. All of these, I couldn't have done it alone. Andre was the man who stood by my side during my lowest moments. It was as if God had known exactly what I needed in my life.

Together, we navigated the complex realm of real estate, armed with creativity and an unshakable belief in our ability to succeed. We had no safety net, no backup plan, only a burning desire to build something extraordinary out of nothing. And we did.

Our real estate journey, born out of necessity, evolved into a flourishing business empire. We learned to spot opportunities where others saw obstacles, and we realized the true power of creativity and systems. It allowed us to make deals happen, even when we lacked surplus funds or an extensive credit history.

Whenever I hear someone lamenting their lack of capital to start investing, I know that not having money to spare can be a hidden blessing. It forces you to think outside the box, be resourceful, and do your homework before diving headfirst into ventures.

As we grew and gained experience, financial institutions began to take notice. Our portfolio expanded, and we ventured into larger projects, including construction and ground-up developments in the Greater Philadelphia area. The financial freedom we attained allowed us to travel together and gain a broader perspective of the world. I also had more time to invest in my passions. Drawing from my experiences as an immigrant, I started taking on volunteer positions in the local community. Currently, I proudly serve as the President of the Korean American Chamber of Commerce for Greater Philadelphia, which has broadened my understanding of various facets of business, beyond just real estate. I've come to appreciate the importance of advocacy and representation. I now understand how financial power and freedom can have a meaningful impact on disadvantaged individuals. Throughout my life, I've sought guidance and clarity in understanding my purpose on this Earth. I believe that God has been guiding us toward a path filled with purpose and significance. This journey has been marked by trials and tribulations, but it has also been illuminated by moments of profound growth and transformation.

As I reflect on the challenges I've faced and the choices I've made, I'm reminded of the strength that faith and determination can provide. It was during those darkest hours in the hospital room, as I grappled with decisions that felt impossible, that I truly discovered the depth of my resilience and adaptability.

I've come to realize that life's most valuable lessons often emerge from unexpected places. The pain of loss and the trials of my early years in a new country served as catalysts for personal and professional growth. My journey, though filled with hardships, has shaped me into the person I am today.

The journey from that hospital room, where my father fought his last battle, to this point in my life was a path I could have never anticipated. As I reflect on my journey, I invite you to consider your own path in life. Embrace resilience, have faith in your abilities, and

recognize the importance of community. Remember that unexpected challenges can lead to the most profound growth.

Susan Noh

Susan Noh is a seasoned real estate investor and developer, known for her prominent presence in the Philadelphia real estate market since 2014. Together with her husband Andre, Susan embarked on her real estate journey, initially starting with real estate wholesaling and gradually building their portfolio through innovative financing strategies, primarily focusing on residential properties. Their dedication and expertise eventually led them to engage in ground-up development and complete full-gut rehab projects, diversifying their investments into multifamily and mixed-use commercial properties.

What sets Susan apart is her remarkable journey from being an immigrant from Korea at the age of 16 to becoming a successful entrepreneur and real estate maven. Her resilience and determination have been the driving forces behind her achievements.

Beyond her real estate ventures, Susan is a visionary entrepreneur who established a short-term rental management company, seamlessly integrating with her diverse real estate portfolio that spans from Philadelphia to the Jersey Shore.

Susan's heart lies in empowering women and minority investors in the real estate industry. She is committed to breaking down barriers and creating opportunities for underrepresented individuals. Her current aspiration is to acquire larger commercial properties and delve into commercial development projects, solidifying her position as a trailblazer in the field.

In addition to her business endeavors, Susan proudly serves as the President of the Korean American Chamber of Commerce for Greater Philadelphia. This role allows her to give back to the Korean American small business community, promoting economic growth and collaboration in the region. With her remarkable journey and unwavering commitment, Susan Noh continues to leave a significant impact on both the real estate and business communities.

linktr.ee/susannoh

PowerfulFemaleImmigrants.com

STUCK IN AN INESCAPABLE MOVIE

Lorraine Chai, Malaysia

I wondered around the roads of Sydney aimlessly towards my car. Did it really happen to me? I went home and took a long hot shower. I had to wash it all off. Maybe if I slept and woke up, it would have all been just a dream… I can't believe I'm hearing myself say this - I was raped. Raped, by not just one man, but five men, and one of them was someone from church whom I thought I could trust.

Overcoming Sexual Assault

Through my journey, I found that three out of five women have been sexually assaulted in their lifetime. The assault is normally carried out by a friend or someone close to the victim. The first reaction of the female victim is to internalize the shame by projecting self-blame and hatred. I've learned that it is never healthy to blame oneself and we should not allow the culprit to trap us in that space of darkness. Many fall into a downward spiral of shame, blame and self-hatred, robbing their peace of mind and joyful life for months or even years.

For me, I addressed my fear, guilt, and pain on my own even though I wanted to disappear and hide from the world. I had made a promised to my late grandmother that I would make her proud. That I would be strong and change the world by helping millions of people find their way out of this same black hole. I decided that I am not a victim but a victor in my life and my future and nothing will stop me. Not even these men. I share my strength and coach women how to overcome themselves and transforming their lives like a phoenix rising from the ashes.

I help women design a life that they desire and stretch their mind towards the vision of the future they deserve. Many may think that they've done the therapy work to overcome their past are not aware that a part of them are still subconsciously stuck to their past and continue attracting abusive men to try to fix their family of origin or their younger self. But when working with me, women learn to strengthen their minds and designing their future with the art of attracting the 'right stuff' into their lives. I have helped many redesign their inner programming to creating a beautiful life that they truly deserve.

My desire is to see women set free in every area of their life - spiritually, emotionally, mentally, physically, and financially.

Music Was My Life

Growing up with a musical mother, it was my birthright that music should be a part of me. Mom introduced me to the piano the moment I should crawl. At age six, mom decided that violin should be my next instrument and by age seven, I had given my first violin performance. I was a very introverted child and often lose myself for hours in playing and writing music. Music was my friend, my identity, my constant companion, and my life. When life got crazy, I had my music - a place I could express myself without judgement. A place I could be somebody else. My world was made believe but it kept me going. It kept me dreaming. It kept my soul dancing from within. Music became my escape, my joy, and mylove.

Teaching Music

I never thought myself ever becoming a teacher. At age fourteen, I decided to give my local community the chance to learn an instrument for free through the church. I recruited musicians and started teaching them how to teach the violin to students effectively and founded a string ensemble. From there, teaching became my passion, my first career transition. Musicians are like athletes where they have to understand the physique of our body in order to not physically harm themselves through repetitive practice. I was great in understanding the mechanism of things and explaining it to others in a language they understood. This skill has helped me through any work I took especially with coaching in helping my clients understand themselves in a straightforward manner to fast-track their personal and professionalgrowth.

He was The One

So, I hoped… I was being smothered. I could not escape. I was in a relationship that sucked all the oxygen out of the room and out of my soul. It made the loneliness in my soul cry out for validation but there was none. Silence…., nothing but silence. He was talking but, I could not hear. He was yelling but, I only heard silence. After being trapped for so long, I learned how to numb myself and withdraw from all the rants and screaming demands.

I was paralyzed. Paralyzed by fear, paralyzed by my own childhood trauma, by my own isolation. I had painted myself into an imaginary corner that was so real it had become a prison, a dark tiny prison with a massive steel door with my hands cuffed and my feet chained to the floor. I couldn't bare it. I felt like a hallow shell. Why should I continue to exist to constantly be treated and feel like this? I wanted to die. Things had spiralled down so deep that all I knew was triggers, traumas, pain, and fear.

Even after the breakup. I was being stalked. He was exhibiting strange and illegal behavior to try and destroy my life. Even his own father was concerned for my safety. But I stuck to my innocence. I fought for a year for my life through the legal system and eventually won. He was not allowed to come within 15 feet to where I was. Although I had my life back, I still had nightmares and was living with fear. Then one day, on Christmas Day, at the age of 49, he was dead. He died of a heart attack, and I was free. A weight of the world lifted off my shoulders.

Or was I?

Stalked by Fear

I had three relationships, where one after the other, read like a horror movie. In one of them, the lights were all turned off. The blinds were all down and I was home alone in darkness with my dog. A loud BANG! BANG! on the door. My ex became my stalker. He learned how to by-pass security to get to the level of my apartment. He would follow me to my work places to vandalise my car wheels and memorised my daily schedule to find any opportunity he could in defaming me in front of the church, at my work places, and within my community. I received threatening emails with no signature where the police would not take any action besides writing a police report.

That was the story of my life. It felt like I had been living in this movie for so long. I could not rest. I lived with a heightened sense of panic and instability.

Losing Your Stalker

When my ex-boyfriend, stalker died, I felt guilty as I knew that one way or another, I caused his death. But I also felt a sense of relief.

Although his physical being no longer lives, I still felt like I was living on the edge ready to act on any possible danger. It bothered me how I couldn't trust people and had a lot of self-doubt. I didn't realized how hyper alert I had become thinking of my own safety and always looking over my shoulder. It affected my health and my emotional well-being for so many months and years. I had to reprogram my mind and set myself free from this chapter of my life. I started by deciding not to let his abuse and his memory haunt me and prevent me from living my life and following my dreams. He said many hurtful and cruel things to me, but I chose to believe in myself and have it not affect me from reaching my goals. I pitied him in his mental illness and decline as he deteriorated quickly during the duration of the court trials. I could not save him and had accepted that I had to be in defensive mode to protect myself. I stayed in this relationship for 3 years as I initially thought that I was the problem. I realized that I felt that way because all my life, I was constantly told by people around me that I was the problem no matter how hard I tried to be the perfect person. After months of reflecting, I realize that I have always put in the effort in the relationship, and that I was in the right. It was a difficult thing for me to do but I gathered all the courage I had within me and decided to break up and never look back. I decided that I am worth more than the way he treated me and I deserved better. I learned to love myself and became strong for myself with the vision I had for my future life. I felt a sense of relief when he passed away, but it still took me time to relax and trust people again.

Finding My Purpose

As a 5-year-old, I saw a lot of sadness and pain in the world and felt like it was my duty to do something about it. I would pray myself to sleep every night that God would help me understand the world to be able to help people find themselves and be able to live in freedom and happiness. I did not truly understand that as a 5-year-old but that was what I always wanted to do. I would always be a part of any visitations to old-folks home or the orphanages or fund-raising musical programs just to see the faces of those people light up.

Looking back at my life, it feels like God gave me the first-hand experience to go through the chapters of my life as he knew I had the strength to overcome them when many would give up. I saw myself as a beacon of light in helping millions of people find themselves and bring them over to this amazing side of life. The path to fulfilment is most often not linear. Life has twists and turns and is filled with speed bumps, flat tires, and dead ends. It's not a question of if but a question of when these setbacks happen, how will you respond? Faith and hope havealways been a big part of my life and I could not make sense of life and manage without my faith, hope for a better future, and the vision of the life I keep seeing myself in. Faith for a better futureand hope that it will soon come intoform.

My Non-Profit and My Trip to Nepal

My life has taught me that I should follow my heart and make the best out of everything that I did. A colleague told me that I should not even consider doing non-profits until I earn more money.

Bullshit!! Around the same time, another colleague mentioned that I should put a high price on my educational books when I wanted it to be accessible and affordable to all. I was fired up and determined to be better than them in making my dream of my non-profit project happen. I used my skills and own resources and made it happen this year with the vision of this eventually turning it into an organization with a strong team to running it. I wanted to give a chance to kids to explore the possibility of so much more out there with the vision that it would spark a light in creating future leaders, educators, and life changing advocates to continue touching more lives.

I started my Non-Profit Music Education Project with Heartland Academy in Kathmandu, Nepal as the first destination where I was blessed to receive donations to support part of this project from companies and individuals all over the world. I started a string program and I sponsored to train two local teachers to continue with the program independently and successfully. It was very rewarding putting instruments into these kids 'hands and seeing the proud joy on the kid's faces when they realized that they were making beautiful music together! Within hours, you could see the kids who have never seen or touch these instruments play so well. Their burning desire to learn more with enthusiasm and gratitude. How I transported 15 instruments and my books into the country is another story for another book, but the challenge and experience was worth the price, and I'll do it again and again.

Beyond the Looking Glass

I see potential in every person I see. The only thing is an individual needs to made that decision to want the change and to do whatever it takes to reaching it. As you have read part of my story, I've lived it all. My duty is to give you that knowledge and showing you the possibility of more. If I can change my traumatic life from an absolute introvert to becoming who I am today and more, so can you. Bet on yourself and take that step forward. Your true life, is calling out to you. What are you waiting for?

"Being mentored by Lorraine was an incredibly rich experience for me. Her guidance transcended the brief set by our partnership – to become a support person as a music industry professional. She empowered me to change aspects of my life that no longer served me. The experience was motivational, prompting the realization that I am already equipped with the skills and strength to achieve my goals. I am very grateful to Lorraine for this mentorship." - Katie B.

Speaking

Since stepping out of my comfort zone as an extreme introvert, speaking has been a part of me which Speaking has always been a passion of mine, and it's something that I've honed over the years. Initially, I found great joy in one-on-one interactions with my students. However, I soon realized that I could make a more significant impact by taking my message to a larger audience, whether on a physical or virtual stage. The COVID-19 pandemic presented a unique opportunity for me to embrace technology and connect with students worldwide. During these challenging times, I used online platforms to share my knowledge to teachers, and teach music to students as well as inspire hundreds of women across the globe through podcasts and virtual summits. This digital shift not only allowed me to reach new clients but also opened doors to lucrative contracts, enabling me to expand my businesses further and reaching more people. It was a transformative experience that showed me the immense potential of leveraging technology for education andoutreach.

Coaching

One of the most rewarding aspects of my work is personally coaching women in various aspects of their lives. I offer a range of coaching services tailored to empower and uplift women, and I wanted to briefly touch on a few of them:

Life Leadership Strategies: Through this coaching, I help women navigate life's challenges, make confident decisions, and take control of their futures.

Relationship Coaching: Building and maintaining healthy relationships is crucial, and I provide guidance to women seeking to strengthen their connections with loved ones.

Transformational Mindset Coaching: For those feeling stuck in life, I offer guidance to help individuals achieve their dreams by breaking free from limitations and taking full control of the mind to go beyond in achieving all the "impossible".

Confidence Coaching: Boosting self-confidence is a transformative journey, and I work closely with women to help them regain their self-esteem and assertiveness in just a few months.

"Highly recommended. I didn't think things were possible until I joined Lorraine's program. She changed my life. Thank you!" - Sara M.

Creating a Legacy

I've always wanted to create something that would live beyond my life and strive to do that every day. So far, I've written 23 books and plan to write many more. If you found me through this book and are feeling stuck, go to my site now and get a FREE copy of 3-Steps to Unleash Your Super Power or book a FREE Strategy Call on the link below.

Lorraine Chai

Lorraine is a world-class coach, international educator, author, speaker, and the Founder of The Empoweress and Stringstastic.

Coming from an artistic, entertainment as a multi-instrumentalist, and over 20 years of teaching experience, Lorraine has always loved being able to support educators and students to embrace themselves in learning differently and be confident in their abilities to the best that they can be. Her recent Non-Profit Music Education Project with Heartland Academy in Kathmandu, Nepal this year is the first of many where she has started a string program and sponsored to train 2 local teachers to continue with the program independently.

Lorraine's love for learning and growing led her to embracing herself and created a drive to seek growth. She seeked out to being mentored by the top, respectable people in the world such as Bob Proctor, Grant Cardone, and Arash Vossoughi . Although known in the music education industry internationally, her love and passion for people led her to coaching. She is passionate about inspiring and empowering women and entrepreneurs to bet on themselves and discover their purpose in life to live in freedom, and embracing their fierce and resilient nature. She empowers women to shape the future which they desire and deserve.

It is never, ever too late to achieve your dream life and live a life of freedom. Anything is possible if you truly believe in it. As Napoleon Hill says *"Cherish your vision and your dreams as they are the children of your soul, the blueprints of your ultimate achievements."* Lorraine is here to help you through that journey to celebrate your achievements with you. So, what are you waiting for?

Connect with Lorraine via

lorrainechai.ccard.to/ and *PowerfulFemaleImmigrants.com*

SCAMMED IN THE USA: A JOURNEY OF RESILIENCE AND EMPOWERMENT

Yuwen "Wendy" Juan, Taiwan

I was just 15 years old when I started ninth grade in the United States, filled with excitement about the land of opportunity and dreams. This was where Disneyland existed, after all.

I came here from Taiwan, not as one of those immigrants with deep pockets, but with my family, seeking a better life. We had investor visas and dreams of a successful business venture. We even had relatives in the country to guide us. Initially, everything seemed promising. I was enrolled in high school, earning good grades, and it felt like we were on the right track. Our investment landed us at a motel where we had to manage it 24/7 and even live their part of the time. I cleaned motel rooms, and my brother pulled the linens and did laundry while my dad was the repair man and he and my mom ran the front office and marketing.

This was just the beginning, because our immigration status made us vulnerable, easy targets for those looking to take advantage of us. Our business venture turned into a disaster, resulting in significant financial losses. Even worse, we realized that we might have been scammed by the attorneys who mishandled our immigration paperwork, leaving us without the visas or green cards we had expected.

Our descent into hardship and uncertainty began. Our once-promising journey took a dark turn, leaving us out of status and financially depleted within a few years. I had one sibling, a brother, and our lives were dramatically altered by these events.

I vividly remember the fear and uncertainty that gripped me during this time. I was on the verge of attending The University of Texas at Austin, and I worried about paying for tuition, whether my admission would be rescinded due to my status, and what the future held.

My initial outgoing nature from Taiwan was gradually replaced by introversion in the US. I became reserved, feeling like I had so much to learn and observe. I hesitated to share my stories, as there was a lot of drama and challenges that came with them. Subconsciously I was always looking over my shoulder to be sure I was not being followed by immigration officials wanting to deport us. It was a huge emotional toll at every level not just on me but on all four of us.

Our financial struggles worsened over time. It wasn't long before we faced the possibility of homelessness, and I found myself in the position of having to ask relatives for loans just to cover our family's disaster. While I resented my parents putting me in this awkward position, I was chosen to make the calls for help and had no choice but to comply. That would put a wedge in our family that exists to this day.

Marriage Did Not Survive

My parents' marriage didn't survive the stress and strain of our circumstances, leading to a strained relationship between my brother and my father. As the eldest daughter, I became the glue holding our family together, even though my parents no longer spoke to each other.

During these difficulties, I realized that our family could never go back to what it once was. This realization marked a turning point in my life. I had to let go of the hope for their reconciliation and focus on moving forward and improving my future, whatever that might be and forging a pathway for me and my brother's future as bleak as it seemed now.

Graduating University of Texas

After four years of blood, sweat and determination and many miles on my feet serving tables and picking up everyone's shift I graduated. I never went on school trips, participated in extracurricular activities, or had serial boyfriends in college. I was busy burning the midnight oil day and night trying to keep my head above water and stay in school with a decent GPA. Walking across that stage with my diploma was an awesome feeling and I felt only a little relieved that my future would improve I would still be driven by fear, hustle, and pure instinct.

With my degree in Fashion Design and my determination that had become habit in the trail and adversity that would be my epic college memory fueled my passion to launch into my dream. My dream of launching my clothing brand in New York City.

Starting over in a new city, the Big Apple really appealed to me. It was a chance to leave behind the hell that had become my life and start with a clean slate.

I was determined, I thought, "This is it. I've got to do this." Money was tight, just enough to rent an apartment for a couple of months. The first thing I bought with that little money was a fax machine so I could send my resume out non-stop.

One Way Ticket to New York City

All day, every day, I'd send those faxes. And finally, I landed a job. I was ecstatic! But you'd think that was my ticket to freedom, right?

I had worked hard to build my career in the fashion industry, climbing the ranks until I became the Vice President of Design. After a few years of working tirelessly, trying to establish my career, even working on Christmas, I realized that this guy was...

Draining my bank account.

I had burned my bridges so to speak and needed to make this hustle work, my parents were not rich, they were not even together. I had to make my career work in the USA I had to do it for me, I had to do it for my brother and me! I'd soon find out life had other plans.

Tying the Knot in The Big Apple

You see, I met this guy back at UT. We started dating, and he said, "You don't have to go alone. I'll go to New York with you. We can get married for your green card, and we'll start our lives in New York." That sounded like a dream. I even thought I loved him. I didn't realize he had other plans. I didn't think about him harming me, I mean sure he was helping me get my green card, but he loved me too, right? At least he said he did when we were dating in college.

I was working so hard, 80 hours a week or more every week plus weekends and holidays. I wasn't paying attention to what was going on with my marriage. He had my social security number and had taken out several credit cards in my name and would intercept them in the mail before I got home from work. When I finally realized what was going on I was tens of thousands of dollars in debt with no way to pay these cards back, even though I had risen in ranks to Executive VP of the Fashion company and launched my own brand I was only making $18,000 per year. It was unfathomable to comprehend HOW he could hurt me like this and WHY I was liable even though HE was the one that ran up the debts without my knowledge.

I'm looking at bank statements and credit card bills, surviving on ramen. He's out there, wining and dining other women with my credit cards, day after day.

Two years into the marriage and on the advice of a divorce attorney who was generous enough to give me a free consultation I was told, "you've got to file for separation, move him out and get a divorce…that's the only way you can put this behind you…"

I had to get out of that situation, I had to declare bankruptcy, all by myself. I didn't even know how to divorce someone. I could not afford the attorney, he put me in touch with the books I needed to read at the library, it was before the internet. I had no one to call. I was entirely on my own, so I went to the library every day and learned how to file for a divorce.

And you won't believe this—he wouldn't even sign the divorce papers.

I told him I needed a divorce. He wouldn't give it to me. He wouldn't show up at the attorney's office, wouldn't sign the divorce decree. I said, "You don't even need to see me. Just go to the doorman and sign this document." He refused. I didn't know what to do.

Years went by, and all I could think was that maybe, just maybe, that piece of paper would be with me when I found him. It never left my purse, wherever I went. I prayed it would and…

Finally…Getting Closure and Moving On!

One day, I was out for lunch, and believe it or not, I saw him! He was on a date. I marched right over, pulled the divorce decree out of my purse, and forced him to sign it on the spot! I had no other options; this was my miracle, and it worked. I was finally free! It played out exactly the way I rehearsed it in my mind a thousand times before. This was my dream, my wish and what I visualized – I couldn't believe it was FINALLY happening! I felt 100% relief. I could finally get closure and move on with my life, I was no longer anyone's wife, and no one could ever screw me over again!

Unbelievable, right? I carried that piece of paper around for so many years. But I didn't give up, and I didn't let him give up either. Eight million people in New York, and I found him!

Yeah, I found him and made him sign that paper right there and then. It's incredible. That was one of the best days of my life. One of the very few.

Maintaining a Winning Mindset

A lot of people would have been derailed by these setbacks but not me. My mindset and desire are strong and when I set my intention,

I begin to attract what I want. It's never easy but I'm a bulldog and I never give up and I ALWAYS win!

And, when something goes wrong, I know I can figure it out. I've done it before. The key is not getting caught up in short-term setbacks. Things may look bleak and negative now but there are people out there who will help you, and most importantly, you've got to help yourself. Believe in yourself, always believe in yourself and your goals. If your goals are honorable, you need patience, determination, ask for help and you will come out on top!

Launching Another Successful Career

I had reached the top of the corporate ladder in the fashion industry and launched my own clothing brand despite all the personal turmoil going on in my life. That was a goal I could check off my list and feel good about. I was not longing for the long hours after I hit my goals and knew the price it would take to stay on top in the fickle world of fashion, so I exited at a good time. I needed something that had more predictable long-term income, I needed something that would help me produce wealth. But not just wealth for me, wealth for many others. I was finally ready to launch into commercial real estate!

Generating Long-Term Wealth with Real Estate

I decided to pursue a career in real estate and earned my license. Over a span of five years, I became a top broker in the industry. Real estate not only provided me with financial stability but also allowed me to help other women, particularly divorced women, regain their financial independence through real estate investments.

One of the most rewarding aspects of my career is witnessing these women rebuild their lives and achieve financial security. They no longer need to rely on anyone else to provide for them. It's a testament to the resilience of the human spirit and the power of determination.

My journey has taught me that life is a continuous journey with no fixed destination. Even in the face of adversity and setbacks, I've learned to focus on solutions and remain solution oriented. It's this mindset that has allowed me to overcome challenges and build the life I want.

My call to action is simple: if you find yourself facing similar challenges or looking to invest in real estate, connect with me. I'm here to share my experiences, provide guidance, and help you achieve financial independence through real estate.

Let's Connect Up and Talk

As I look back on my life, I realize that every obstacle and setback has shaped me into the person I am today. I've learned that it's not about avoiding challenges but about how we choose to respond to them. With determination, resilience, and the willingness to seek solutions, we can overcome even the most daunting obstacles and create the future we desire.

Join me on this journey, and together, we can empower ourselves and others to rise above adversity and thrive in the face of challenges. Life is a journey, and I'm excited to continue exploring it with you.

Connect with me on Instagram @_Wendy_Juan and schedule a call to explore how real estate can be a path to financial independence. Your future is waiting, and I'm here to guide you on your journey.

Yuwen "Wendy" Juan is a dynamic professional with a remarkable journey that spans across diverse industries and continents. With a passion for real estate and a successful career as a real estate agent and investor in the bustling metropolis of New York City, Yuwen has proven herself as a valuable resource in the world of property investment.

Originally hailing from a tranquil village in Taiwan, Yuwen's upbringing was marked by the values of hard work and ambition instilled by her parents. Her mother, a teacher, and her father, a business owner, moved the family to the United States in pursuit of a better life. Yuwen's American journey began in Texas, where she started high school and embarked on a path that would eventually lead her to New York City.

Before entering the real estate arena, Yuwen spent over two decades as a renowned fashion designer, jet-setting around the globe and immersing herself in the world of style and creativity. Her love for travel and diverse cultural experiences has enriched her perspective and made her a true global citizen.

With a loving family that includes her two sons, a supportive husband, and a rescued dog, Yuwen Juan has found balance between her personal and professional life. Today, she channels her wealth of experience and dedication to help individuals especially women achieve financial freedom and success in the world of real estate, just as she has done herself. Yuwen Juan's story is one of resilience, adaptability, and unwavering commitment to her goals, making her a true inspiration to those she works with.

Yuwen "Wendy" Juan

Yuwen Juan is a dynamic professional with a remarkable journey that spans across diverse industries and continents. With a passion for real estate and a successful career as a real estate agent and investor in the bustling metropolis of New York City, Yuwen has proven herself as a valuable resource in the world of property investment.

Originally hailing from a tranquil village in Taiwan, Yuwen's upbringing was marked by the values of hard work and ambition instilled by her parents. Her mother, a teacher, and her father, a business owner, moved the family to the United States in pursuit of a better life. Yuwen's American journey began in Texas, where she started high school and embarked on a path that would eventually lead her to New York City.

Before entering the real estate arena, Yuwen spent over two decades as a renowned fashion designer, jet-setting around the globe and immersing herself in the world of style and creativity. Her love for travel and diverse cultural experiences has enriched her perspective and made her a true global citizen.

With a loving family that includes her two sons, a supportive husband, and a rescued dog, Yuwen Juan has found balance between her personal and professional life. Today, she channels her wealth of experience and dedication to help individuals especially women achieve financial freedom and success in the world of real estate, just as she has done herself. Yuwen Juan's story is one of resilience, adaptability, and unwavering commitment to her goals, making her a true inspiration to *those she works with.*

instagram.com/_wendy_juan

PowerfulFemaleImmigrants.com

MY PURPOSE: A JOURNEY FROM SELF-HATRED TO SELF-LOVE

Roushel Eid, Phillipines

Let me begin my life story by acknowledging that it's not a unique one. There was no cataclysmic event that altered the course of my life, no miraculous moment that instantly transformed me. Just like yours, my life is a series of events that have shaped who I am today, marked by challenges, self-hatred, and self-doubt that I've wrestled with throughout and still confront today. Overcoming these crippling negativities has been a significant part of my journey.

Growing up in the quaint, picturesque mountain city of Baguio in the Philippines, I was the eldest in a single-parent household. Growing up, my identity seemed overshadowed by the ridicule and contempt that engulfed my formative years. I was filled with hate, not for others, but for myself. Words of scorn had etched themselves onto my soul, and I believed every negative comment about my appearance defined my worth.

I can vividly recall being young, feeling loved and accepted by everyone around me. In my early youth, fear was virtually nonexistent, and nothing seemed to stop me. However, as life unfolded, I entered the challenging phase of adolescence. Acne plagued my face, becoming a source of humiliation. My once dark skin turned even darker, and my thick, unruly hair seemed uncontrollable. Adding to my insecurities, I gained weight, and my growth stunted. Meanwhile, my younger sister, my female cousins, and my friends blossomed into perfect individuals. All of them, it seemed, had lean, slender figures, smooth, fair skin, soft hair, and perfect noses. I hated being in groups, much less photos, with any of them, as my imperfections became amplified next to these perfect young ladies, fueling my feelings of inadequacy.

Suddenly, my appearance became the measuring stick by which everyone judged me. In a culture that idolized Western beauty standards, it felt like an unattainable goal to change my appearance. I internalized the belief that because I didn't fit this narrow mold of beauty, I wouldn't be successful, and opportunities would be limited due to my height and other physical attributes.

Unsolicited comparisons started pouring in from both family and strangers. While these comments may have been innocent or merely observational, they seared into my self-image and self-respect like burning embers. I was also already grappling with multiple stressors in my life, from my parents separating to the passing of my father, who left behind a trail of mistresses and failed businesses. All these incidents seemed to converge, burdening my life even further.

"Oh my god, what happened to you?" – as if my appearance was a result of some chemical reaction.

"Why don't you look like your sister?" Hold on, let me ask my mother.

"Who did you piss off to come out like that?" I desperately wanted to know what that meant.

"Your legs are so thick you must be embarrassed to be seen wearing shorts!" I wondered what I should wear during the hot summer months.

"Roushel, you should not be wearing that; it shows your fat arms!" The comments were relentless.

"We regret to inform you that you did not meet the criteria to be accepted to the College of Nursing." I was turned away because I did not meet the height requirement, despite possessing high grades.

School offered no sanctuary; instead, I endured incessant taunting and bullying from my classmates because I was tiny. One fateful day, as I walked home, three kids cornered me, showering me with punches and kicks. It was like something out of a movie, an unthinkable reality I never anticipated facing. Another painful incident occurred during my audition for a dance club. Despite weeks of dedicated practice, I overheard supposed friends from the club mocking my performance, asserting that I moved like a goat. These experiences left me questioning everything. Why was I subjected to such treatment? What was wrong with me? Why did people harbor so much animosity towards me? Did God intend for me to be unloved and unwanted? Why was I even born?

This marked a pivotal moment for me; I finally grasped the cruel and unfriendly nature of the world. It seemed there was no other explanation - good people indeed finished last. By the time I entered high school, I had transformed into a bully. It may be hard to believe, but this short, pudgy girl was terrorizing her school and getting away with it. I adopted the belief that if people didn't like me, they would at least fear me. My academic performance gave me a sense of power, and I used it to humiliate others, belittling them for their failures and low grades. It was the first time I felt a semblance of control and dominance.

As college approached, I knew I needed to employ the same survival technique that had served me well before. I had my sights set on a sorority, but not just any sorority—the one that commanded respect on campus, known for its rigorous hazing rituals. Over the course of twelve weeks, I went through intense hazing designed to break down my ego. I endured public humiliation, mental games, and physical beatings. Family and friends asked why I chose to be a part of this organization. I wanted to scream, "They are the only ones who will take me as their own!" But I just shrugged and kept quiet.

Honestly, I can't deny that there were moments after the initiation when I felt accepted, like I had found my tribe. But the harsh reality is that to belong, I had to pay a price. My involvement in pledge-hazing created a cycle of violence that I never wanted to be a part of.

Throughout my college years, I drifted aimlessly. My relationship with my family turned sour, and my childhood friends no longer seemed to align with who I was becoming. My mom had left for the UK to find work, while I irresponsibly squandered the allowance she sent for me and my sister. I started drinking heavily and spent my nights in clubs, leading me to develop unhealthy habits that made me lose weight and look emaciated. I felt like I was spiraling out of control, but I had no idea how to break free from the downward spin.

Against the odds, I managed to graduate on time, but deep down, I knew that if I wanted to change my life, I had to leave my hometown. I found a job at a call center agent in Manila, which took me seven hours away from Baguio. However, even in this new city, I felt trapped in a meaningless existence. I lacked purpose and reasons to keep going, with seemingly no opportunity to create a better life for myself. Despite attempting to find better jobs where I could excel, I always seemed to be overlooked because I didn't have strong connections or fit certain beauty standards. By the age of 23, bitterness and defeat had become all too familiar.

An incredible opportunity presented itself when I received the news that I could travel to the US. The excitement within me was overwhelming. It was my chance to escape the country that had abandoned me and start afresh. However, apprehension crept in too. The US is often seen as the epitome of Western beauty standards, where certain physical attributes are deemed the norm. The fear of being judged based on appearances haunted me as I prepared for the journey. I knew I had to strategize on how to handle potential critics and earn respect, all while creating opportunities for myself in this new land.

To my surprise, things didn't unfold as I expected. Upon arrival, I was met with warm welcomes from friends and family, and even strangers and neighbors seemed kinder. Doubts lingered, but I decided to embrace the experience with an open heart.

The diversity of the US made me feel less like an outsider. Witnessing people who looked like me thriving in their lives and succeeding in their careers and businesses opened my eyes to the possibilities ahead. America truly lived up to its reputation as the land of opportunities, especially for those willing to take risks. I soon discovered that appearances were not as crucial as how people presented themselves, and little by little, I started shedding my inhibitions.

A newfound fire began to burn within me. The love and acceptance I received from others had a profound impact on my relationship with myself. Passion ignited where there was once none, propelling me to step out of my comfort zone, make friends, and form genuine bonds with others. As I began to like and trust myself more, I noticed positive changes happening within me.

I took charge of my destiny and set out to prove everyone, including myself, wrong. Joining a dance class marked my first step, and soon, I found myself becoming the standout dancer in the group. It was hard to believe when strangers approached me to compliment my rhythm – me, the same person who was once rejected from the high school dance club. With newfound confidence, I decided to share my love for dance by teaching Zumba, a fusion of dance and exercise. Not only did it help me maintain a healthy weight, but it also allowed me to empower girls who struggled with body image. Witnessing their transformations during our classes and seeing sparks of self-love in their eyes when they danced and looked in the mirror filled me with joy. At last, I had discovered my purpose.

I also chose to pursue nursing, leaving behind the distant memory of rejection from a nursing school in the Philippines. Gaining admission to a nursing program was fiercely competitive, but I dedicated myself wholeheartedly to the cause, determined not to give the admission officials any reason to deny me. Through hard work and perseverance, I earned my nursing degree and have now been practicing for over a decade, serving proudly as a nurse leader in critical ICUs in northern California. My height no longer mattered as it once did, and my appearance played no role in how I cared for my patients or saved lives. I knew my true purpose in my role, and everything else became mere background noise. I climbed the ranks in my department through unwavering dedication to the profession, the patients I served, and the colleagues I proudly called my battle buddies.

Through my dedication to nursing, I ventured into new business endeavors - The Cashflow Nurse and Eid Equity. These ventures aim to empower nurses and healthcare professionals by helping them build wealth and generate passive income through multifamily and commercial real estate.

Now, I navigate life with self-love and acceptance. I've learned that if an opportunity is denied to me, I have the power to create my own. My worth and potential are not determined by my appearance or others' opinions of me; instead, they are rooted in my sense of purpose. Looking back, it feels like a whole lifetime has passed since I left the Philippines almost two decades ago. The person I am today is vastly different from who I was back then.

Looking ahead, I envision becoming a mother one day. I have made a solemn vow to empower my children from an early age, celebrating their uniqueness and reassuring them that they belong in this world. I will teach my children that the world isn't inherently cruel, though some people may be unkind. Yet, their meanness will never define my children's worth. Together, we will visit Baguio, a place that holds my childhood pain. It will serve as a reminder that the beginning does not determine one's path; what truly matters is the person one becomes despite all odds.

Roushel Eid

In 2004, Roushel Eid made the bold decision to immigrate from the Philippines with nothing but determination, grit, and tenacity. She worked her way up the corporate ladder first as a nurse recruiter in a nurse staffing company to branch manager in 4 years. in 2008 she decided to pursue nursing and despite not having the funds, facing tremendous self-doubt, she persevered and put herself through school with honors. Today with 13 years of nursing experience under her belt, Roushel has risen to become a nurse leader at a well-known academic hospital in Palo Alto, California, where Roushel championed nurse-centered causes and established a mentorship program, increasing nurse retention on her unit.

Her drive for self-improvement led her to venture into real estate investing with her husband. Together, they built a business of single-family long-term rentals before transitioning to multifamily real estate investing. In just eight months, they built their portfolio to 503 units both as passive and active investors. Roushel has seen the power of Multifamily Investments in wealth building and is determined to share this knowledge with her fellow nurses through her company The Cashflow Nurse which provides valuable education on real estate investing.

Behind her incredible journey is the unwavering love and support from her husband Tarek, sister Ann and mother Celenia. She also gives credit to her aunts Aida and Marie for their generosity that helped her get started as an immigrant. To learn more about her inspiring story you can reach her at

roushel@thecashflownurse.com

PowerfulFemaleImmigrants.com

WHAT IS A WOMAN'S MOST VALUABLE ASSET?

Kelli & Mari Ann Nguyen-Ha, Vietnam

Is it GRATEFULNESS?

Is it GENERATIONAL WEALTH? Is it PASSIVE INCOME?

Is it RESIDUAL INCOME?

Is it SELF-EMPOWERMENT? Is it FAMILY?

PLEASE ALLOW TO EXPLAIN MY OWN VERSION…

Introduction

My name is Kelli Nguyen-Ha. Together with my five sisters, Jennifer, Mari Ann, Monica, Melyssa, and Melynda, we are the creators of The FierceSix Mutifamily Equities. Of the six of us, Mariann and I are currently the active members of FierceSix MultiFamily Equities. Our company's mission is to empower one million women by 2033 to take control of their finances, and to help them create passive income through multifamily investing, which will in turn allow them to contribute to the world and become the best providers and givers. With our help, these women will be able to build generational wealth and live the lifestyles of their dreams. The name FierceSix represents the common character amongst the six girls in our family, and how we strive to continuously honor our late parents by working diligently and wisely every day. We relentlessly seek self-improvement and growth, both spiritually and financially, to become better human beings.

I have documented my journey as an immigrant in my first best Amazon's selling book titled, "Immigrant Millionaire: The Story of One Asian Woman Obsessed to Succeed in the Land of Opportunity." We consider ourselves FierceSix Sisters because it is the principles and life values that our late parents instilled in us that made us approach every aspect of our lives with a fearless, can-do attitude of self empowerment.

In my book, I talk about how I got into real estate back in 2008 as a complete beginner with a passion of becoming a millionaire, and in no time had achieved a multimillionaire status. As a family we wanted to achieve financial independence and freedom because it was the only way we would be able to support our loved ones. Our loved ones also include the less fortunate ones back in our native village in Vietnam, in our home state of Texas, and everywhere else in the world. As documented in my book, we are currently donating medicine, and rice for the elderly & the disabled in our ancestral village in Vietnam under our late parents' names. We know this was all possible because of the self empowerment we emulated from our parents.

The Brazilian football (soccer) player, Pelé once said, "*Success is no accident, it is hard work, perseverance, learning, studying, sacrifice and most of all, love of what you are doing or learning to do.*"

Women's Most Valuable Asset- Self Empowerment

In this chapter, I'm going to talk about the most valuable asset you have, which is self empowerment. As FierceSix Sisters, we know that every woman has the innate capability to carry, provide, and empower all the men in our lives. Our grandmothers created our fathers, our mothers-in-law carried our husbands, our moms created our brothers, and we created our sons as individualized and powerful women.

But let me just reiterate that our most valuable asset as women is not the men in our lives, but ourselves. Every one of us must be self-reliant, self-sufficient, and self-dependent. We must be our own heroines and find strength within our own capabilities.

You see, every man has a woman in their life, whether it is their mom, their wife, their sister, or their daughter. And it's easy to lose ourselves in those roles, or to pour all of our time and energy into taking care of others. But the truth is you cannot pour from an empty cup. You must take care of yourself first in order to have the strength and energy to care for others.

Becoming Self Empowered

Believing in Yourself

So, how do you become self-empowered? It starts with believing in yourself. Believe that you are capable of achieving your dreams and goals. Believe that you have the power to overcome any obstacle that comes your way. Believe that you are worthy of love, respect, and success.

In 2008, when I made the decision to pursue a career in real estate, I lacked any prior experience or knowledge in this field. However, I had a strong belief that if others could achieve success in this industry, then I could too. Even if it means that my journey could take twice as long compared to others due to all my inherent barriers as an immigrant and as a 4'11" female playing in the male-dominated world of Business and Commercial Real Estate.

Another favorite quote goes, *"I'm not impressed by your looks, money, social status or job title. I'm impressed by the way you treat other human beings."*

Taking Action

Next, take action. Take steps towards your goals, no matter how small they may seem. Every step forward is progress, and progress leads to momentum. Momentum ultimately leads to success.

Sometimes, though, taking action can be scary. It means stepping out of our comfort zone, and facing your fears. Quite honestly that is where self-empowerment is born. When you are self-empowered, you have the confidence and courage to take action, even when it's difficult.

"F.E.A.R. has two meanings - Forget Everything And Run OR Face Everything And Rise. The Choice is yours." – Zig Ziglar

Taking massive action can be an incredibly empowering experience, particularly when it comes to boosting your confidence level. By diving in and taking action, you give yourself the opportunity to gain first-hand experience and knowledge, which can help to build your self-assurance and self-belief. There is simply no other way to gain this type of experience other than to take the leap and "just do it." While the prospect of taking massive action can be intimidating, particularly when facing a new or challenging situation, the rewards can be tremendous.

Here are four tips on how to become self-empowered:

Define your values and priorities. What is important to you in life? What are your goals and aspirations? When you know what you stand for and what you want to achieve, it becomes easier to make decisions and take action.

Surround yourself with positive influences. Spend time with people who support, encourage you, & who sincerely cares that you succeed. Seek out mentors and role models who have achieved what you aspire to achieve.

Take care of yourself. This means getting enough sleep, eating well, and exercising regularly. It also means taking care of your mental health, practicing self-care, managing stress, and seeking help when you need it.

Embrace your strengths and weaknesses. You are not perfect, and that's okay. Embrace your strengths and use them to your advantage. Acknowledge your weaknesses and work on improving them.

Self Empowerment Is A Journey

It's also important to remember that self-empowerment is not a destination, but a journey. It's something that you must work on every day. There will be ups and downs, successes and setbacks. For me to get to where I am now in life, I almost threw in the towel way too many times. I'd say, the low moments seemed to last forever, but looking back in retrospect I appreciate them as lessons. I can now reflect with a lot of real estate wisdom on the long days when I used to multitask as a room cleaner, breakfast attendant, laundry attendant, front desk clerk, auditor, and any other positions to redevelop a hotel. As recounted in my first book, I did what it took to turn the hotel's less than $300k annual revenue to over $1.2 million in less than three years.

Having Faith In Your Journey

Having faith in your journey is an essential aspect of self-empowerment for women. It means believing in yourself, trusting your intuition, and embracing the challenges and opportunities that come your way. Self-empowerment requires resilience, determination, and the ability to overcome obstacles. It involves taking risks, making mistakes, and learning from them.

By having faith in your journey, you acknowledge that success is not always immediate, and setbacks & obstacles are the lessons designed for you to learn. Instead of being discouraged by failure, we should be empowered by those experiences as opportunities for growth and improvement. When you have faith in your journey, you will be committed to your goals and take the necessary steps to achieve them, leading to a more fulfilling and rewarding life.

My belief in life is: *"Whatever happened to you, happened for a reason & whoever crossed your path, also crossed for a reason"*

Setting and Achieving Goals

One important aspect of self-empowerment is the ability to set and achieve goals. Without goals, we may feel aimless and uncertain about our future. By setting goals and working towards them, we give ourselves direction and purpose. It's important to remember that goals don't have to be big or complex. They can be as simple as learning a new skill or trying a new hobby. The important thing is that we set them for ourselves and work towards them with determination and focus.

Prioritizing Physical and Mental Health

Another key aspect of self-empowerment is self-care. As a retired registered nurse, Certified Critical Care Nurse (CCRN) and Director of Nurses (DON), I highly recommend prioritizing both your physical and mental health. This includes engaging in regular physical activity, such as walking, running, or yoga, to maintain a healthy weight and reduce t risk of chronic illnesses.

In addition, taking care of your mental health is just as important. Try to make time for relaxation and stress-reducing activities, such as meditation or reading a book. Finally, it's essential to get enough sleep each night to help your body and mind rest and rejuvenate.

Standing Up For Yourself

Self-empowerment also means standing up for ourselves and advocating for our own needs. It's unfortunate that throughout my work life, I've faced discrimination from my male counterparts. Most of the time they would dismiss me without even giving me a chance to share my thoughts or contributions.

It was frustrating but I stood up for myself, my colleagues, my team, and what I believed in on many occasions. One incident I also share in my book is confronting a Prominent Cardiac Surgeon who had a habit of undermining female nurses in my department. Trust me, in that very moment when I verbally faced him, I was shaking in my knees and thought I would get fired right away. It took a lot of courage. He changed his ways and became respectful then after.

Your Self Worth

One important aspect of self-empowerment is developing a strong sense of self-worth. Women often struggle with self-esteem issues, especially in a society that puts so much emphasis on physical appearance and traditional gender roles. But we must remember that our worth is not determined by our looks, our job, or our relationships. We are valuable and deserving of respect simply because we exist as human beings.

Setting Boundaries

Another important aspect of self-empowerment is learning to set boundaries and being able to say no when necessary. As women, we often feel the pressure to be people-pleasers, and to put the needs of others before our own. This, however, can lead to a sense of being burned out, resentment, and a sense of powerlessness. By setting boundaries and saying no when we need to, we are respecting our own needs and desires, and sending a message to others that our time and energy are valuable.

It's important to remember that setting boundaries and saying no doesn't make us selfish or mean. It simply means that we are prioritizing our own well-being and recognizing that we can't be everything to everyone all the time.

Taking Responsibility

Self-empowerment also involves taking responsibility for our own actions and choices. It's easy to blame external factors for our problems and limitations, but this mindset leaves us feeling powerless and stuck. By taking responsibility for our own actions and choices, we are acknowledging that we have the power to make changes and to create the life we choose.

Of course, this doesn't mean that we are solely responsible for our circumstances or that we should blame ourselves for things that are out of our control. But it does mean that we can choose how we respond to our circumstances and how to take action to create a better outcome.

Collaborating With Others

One of my all time favorite quotes is an African proverb that says, *"If you want to go fast go alone. If you want to go far go together."*

Self-empowerment involves developing a sense of community and connection with others. As women, we are often socialized to compete with one another and tear each other down, but this only serves to hold us back and prevent us from achieving our full potential.

Instead, we must learn to support and uplift one another, recognizing that when one of us succeeds, we all benefit. This can involve building strong relationships with other women, seeking out mentors and role models, and giving back to our communities in meaningful ways.

Prioritizing Your Finances

It is essential for women to have a steady income source and to be able to manage their finances. This means developing financial literacy and being knowledgeable about investments, savings, and budgeting. Having control over your finances can lead to more freedom and independence, giving you the power to make your own decisions without being reliant on others.

Mentoring

One way to empower others is through mentorship. The two factors that contributed to my success in real estate are mentorships and the unwavering determination that I had. I am a member of multiple businesses. CRE Masterminds and Grant Cardone's CRE Club are just two of the many communities that I currently belong to and continue to be empowered by. I've attended and continue to attend real estate conferences, seminars, local meetups and other events regularly. I am always very grateful for all our mentors throughout my journey. Today, I am giving back what I have gathered from my mentorships to my employees, interested strangers, and even to my two sons to become proficient in all matters.

In Conclusion

As women, we are powerful, resilient, and capable of achieving incredible things. By embracing self-empowerment, we can overcome the barriers that hold us back from achieving our goals and aspirations. I love that one reviewer of my book mentioned that my story reminds us of the incredible potential within each of us, and inspires us to pursue our own paths with courage and determination.

Thus, this is to all the women out there. Remember that your self-empowerment is your most valuable asset. Believe in yourself, invest in your education, build a support system, and don't be afraid to take risks. You have the power to achieve anything you set your mind to, and the world needs your unique and individualized talents and contributions. Go out there and make your mark on the world!

Show the world what a fierce and empowered woman can do!

Kelli & Mari Ann Nguyen-Ha

Kelli Nguyen-Ha is a full-time residential & CRE investor for over 14 years. She currently has $10M+ in Assets Under Management, $10M+ as an investor, and $10M+ in single-family homes and commercial real estate transactions completed full cycle. This is all in addition to 20+ years as a business owner, operator, and manager. As a Wall Street Journal & USA Today featured author, Kelli's first book is a love letter to her roots and parents titled: "Immigrant Millionaire: The Story of One Asian Woman Obsessed to Succeed in the Land of Opportunity."

As an investor, Mari Ann has transacted $2M+ CRE deals and $1M+ land deals. She's been a business owner in the beauty industry for 10+ years and has 20+ years of experience in retail business management. Mariann's expertise is in networking and connecting with people. Jennifer has been a successful business owner and an operator in the retail space for over 30 years. Together with their other three sisters as passive partners, FIERCESIX, INC was born and they are on a mission to create a billion-dollar company by 2033 by helping a million families achieve financial freedom through passive income secured by multifamily assets.

Kelli can be reach at
    KelliNguyenha.com
    PowerfulFemaleImmigrants.com

REINVENTING DREAMS
ONE WOMAN'S ODYSSEY FROM VIETNAM TO VICTORY

Havan Le, Vietnam

Imagine, for a moment, stepping into the dream world of an average American. What do you see? The picture painted is typically an idyllic vision of peace, one of pristine, sun-kissed beaches being gently lapped by azure waters and a retirement devoid of financial stress. The aspiration is the type of retirement where the only hustle is deciding whether the family portrait on the mantlepiece is perfectly aligned or choosing which exotic corner of the world to explore next. To realize such a dream, however, an intimidating sum of at least $1.27 million is perceived as necessary. Reality, often served with a bitter, sarcastic twist, reveals that the savings of most Americans fall severely short of these lofty expectations, as highlighted by the painstaking research conducted by Northwestern Mutual.

Indulge me as we play out a hypothetical scenario. Suppose you're employed in a job that provides the U.S. median salary of $59,428 per year (Bureau of Labor Statistics), and you've managed to master the intricate art of frugality. Every penny you earn is conscientiously saved for the unknown future. Even in this ideal scenario, it would still take you an overwhelming 21 years to accumulate $1.27M. Surely, the difficulty of such a proposition would not be lost on anyone, even a child. Therefore, the critical question arises: if your retirement savings are still a mere speck on the horizon, are you doomed to labor till your last breath? Well, let's pause that thought for a moment and plunge into the depths of my personal narrative, a tale that's been kissed by fortune herself.

The journey that I have embarked upon, captured eloquently within the pages of this book, has been enlivened by the company of 23 other extraordinary women. The day I was brought into this world must have been one when Lady Luck herself was beaming, for I was bestowed a name as unique as Havan Le. In the land of dreams and opportunities, America, many chose to address me by an endearing variation of my name, "Heavenly." Unlike more conventional Vietnamese names such as "Que Chi," "Long Le," or "Phuc Huu," my name provided me with a distinctive identity, setting me apart from the crowd. For this, I offer a heartfelt salute to my mother's creative ingenuity in naming me.

My childhood, set against the vibrant backdrop of Vietnam, was a complicated curtain woven from threads of joy, struggle, and resilience. In a family of four siblings, as the child nestled in the middle, I led a modest existence, often grappling with feelings of being overlooked. Despite the volatile relationship our parents shared, injured by frequent heated exchanges and occasional bouts of physical confrontations, they strived to sustain a pretense of normalcy. It was as though they were seasoned actors playing their roles in a private theater, their performances seeped in years of practice. Men, their judgment often clouded by alcohol, would frequently return home in a stagger, their loud, furious voices echoing off the walls, casting a sinister shadow of tension over our humble household.

As a kid, I held onto the thin hope that dawn might bring a break from the drama – kind of like hoping for sunshine after a week-long thunderstorm in the summertime. Eventually, the constant fighting came to an end with my parents' divorce. My father chose to detach himself from our lives, leaving us four siblings in the sole care of our mother. Thus, we were brought up in a single-parent household, guided and nurtured by our young, resilient mother.

Yet, within this turmoil, I discovered pockets of pure joy and accomplishment. I often found myself in the limelight at beauty and talent contests, both at school and within our province. The stage seemed to spring to life as I walked across it, embellished in beautiful garments painstakingly stitched with love and care by my adoring aunt and eldest sister. If not for that, I would have been dressed in secondhand clothes passed down to me. The admiration of my friends and the praise showered upon me by my teachers painted a rather rosy picture of life.

Life was pure bliss – that is, until the day my mother declared, "We're relocating to the United States!" For many back home in Vietnam, this would have been the equivalent of a fairy tale's happy ending, especially given that we had the rare luxury of boarding an airplane, unlike many refugees who braved treacherous ocean crossings. But for me, it spelled an inner unrest. The abruptness of the move left me with little time to marinate my feelings, and I found myself being practically hauled onto an airplane by my mother. I wouldn't have been surprised if the onlookers mistook the scene for a grand-scale abduction. The sudden shift from the familiar, narrow lanes of Vietnam to an alien land whipped up a storm of emotions within me, though not my three siblings.

Back in my homeland, I was surrounded by a close-knit circle of friends who felt more like family. In contrast, in this strange new country, I was isolated, a solitary figure in a crowd. At 14 years old, grappling with this unfamiliar language known as English was a dreadful task. The incorporation of slang and various other phrases rooted in American culture only amplified my bewilderment, leaving me navigating through a maze of linguistic confusion. The vast discrepancies between the American portrayal of Vietnamese heroes and the history I had grown up with left me in a state of utter confusion. This labyrinth, coupled with an overpowering sense of loneliness, nudged me into my shell, extinguishing my motivation to assimilate into the American culture.

However, amidst these testing times, my mother rose to the challenge of single-handedly steering us through this transitional phase. She demonstrated that change could indeed be a faithful ally, not a foe. Despite our living conditions not seeing any substantial improvement – the five of us crammed into a tiny 10x10 room – we felt a noticeable elevation in our lives. Now, my mother was free from her constant worries about her safety, and the social stigma we had braved back home was a chapter of the past.

We dove into the American way of life from our second day in this new world, working tirelessly to repay the debts we owed to our family members who had supported us in our journey here. During these teenage years, I took on as many jobs as I could manage outside of school hours, all in a bid to contribute to the family's upkeep. My mode of getting to these minimum-wage jobs often involved either walking or hitching a ride.

Luxuries such as dining out were a rarity, as infrequent as a blue moon. Yet, I still vividly remember the day we first stepped into a Golden Corral; it was comparable to stepping into a Rolls Royce Dealership. Fried chicken, meatloaf, and a treasure trove of other mouth-watering delicacies overwhelmed our senses, tossing us into a state of sheer bliss. To this day, that meal, in all its humble glory, remains etched in my memory. It outshines even the most exquisite lobster and the finest steak from around the world.

The hurdles we encountered in this new land were intimidating, but they also instilled in us a robust set of values – the significance of hard work, the inevitable need for perseverance, and the beauty of resilience. It was a rigorous, seemingly never-ending initiation that transformed us into authentic Americans. Our transition was akin to the caterpillar's metamorphosis into a butterfly; the process was challenging, but the outcome was simply beautiful.

One might wonder how an individual hailing from such humble beginnings managed to dance with the elusive dame called success. While it's not a tale of sudden, fantastical windfalls or miraculous interventions, it is an ode to the time-tested principles of diligent work, perseverance, and a dash of entrepreneurial spirit.

It wasn't until I found myself carrying the promise of our firstborn that I felt a surge of desire for more. I yearned to be capable of providing for our parents and bolstering our savings for any unforeseen circumstances. I also nurtured the dream of having a nest egg large enough to purchase our very own home. Most importantly, I desired a life of financial independence. However, the struggle between striving to be the best mother and aiming for financial freedom was immense.

As we journeyed into mid-2015, my husband and I plunged headfirst into the vast ocean of real estate investing. We were admittedly novices, with our personal house being our only exposure to the world of real estate. But change was on the horizon. My husband hoped to break free from constant traveling for work, and I dreamed of building a business that we could nurture together.

In our debut year of business, we surpassed a financial milestone, raking in a profit exceeding $125k. Remarkably, the following year saw us double that profit, then doubling it again in the subsequent year. Indeed, one can accumulate wealth through various avenues such as selling real estate, wholesaling, house flipping, new construction projects, or owning a business. Each of these methods could pave your way to richness. However, the path to sustainable wealth, the kind that leaves a lasting legacy, is predominantly through owning real estate – more precisely, possessing income-generating assets. The more assets you hold, the more zeros you'll see embellishing your financial statement.

Our first long-term investment came in the form of a humble, three-bedroom property named Misty Sands. The property was not a grand estate, nor was it nestled in a lavish locality. Instead, it was a simple, plain construction, settled on a charming location with an appealing view. However, this investment offered us a significant opportunity for value addition. With a modest budget dedicated to refurbishment, we breathed new life into this property, enhancing its appeal and, consequently, its rental value.

The refurbishment was not an overnight endeavor; instead, it was a long-drawn process that involved countless hours of hard work, negotiations, and meticulous planning. However, upon completion, the property shone in a new light, reflecting the labor and love we had poured into it. The tangible result of our efforts was the increased rental income that followed, allowing us to refinance it into a long-term mortgage. This arrangement presented us with an income stream that was essentially the fruit of our own labor.

Our second acquisition was a turnkey property, previously owned by a valued customer. The place was home to long-term tenants who loved their residence, which made the property a reliable source of passive income. In addition, the financial arrangement allowed us to refinance the property into a long-term mortgage, which further solidified our income stream. Unlike Misty Sands, this property didn't require much work, yet it consistently churned out an income for us like a well-oiled machine.

The wisdom conveyed by the legendary investor Warren Buffet holds a special place in our hearts. His saying, "If you don't find a way to make money while you sleep, you will work till you die," is a mantra that has guided us through our journey of investment.

Now, let's take a moment to crunch some numbers. Five properties, each bringing in a neat $200 per month, culminate in an annual income of $12,000. While it may not suffice to finance a lavish retirement, it's a substantial amount, especially when considering its passive nature. These earnings, accrued while we sleep, have been instrumental in elevating our lifestyle, allowing us to indulge in luxuries we once only dreamt of.

In a span of just five years, the property values nearly doubled, allowing us to cash out almost $1M in 2021. This windfall, which was all tax-free courtesy of the marvels of refinancing, was a significant milestone in our investment journey. Today, our investment portfolio has diversified our income streams and proven to be a reliable safety net. The passive income we earn has surpassed our expenses, giving us the freedom to live life on our own terms. If you're interested in learning more, visit my YouTube channel at RealEstateSuperMoms. com. where I share the behind-the-scenes strategies and stories that have led to my success in the real estate industry. I welcome your thoughts, feedback, and personal anecdotes. Consider subscribing if you find value in this story.

With this financial freedom in hand, my new goal is to empower 100,000 women and moms to achieve similar independence through real estate investing. Together, we can validate another of Warren Buffet's iconic quotes, "Never depend on a single source of income; make an investment to create a second source."

As I raise a toast to you, dear reader, for joining me on this journey, I hope that our shared path will illuminate the way to your financial independence. I want my experiences and lessons to serve as a guide, making your journey smoother and more joyful. So, let's step forth, hand in hand, and chase after our dreams, making them a reality in this enchanting world of opportunities.

Havan Le

Based in Houston, TX, Havan Le is not just a dynamic real estate entrepreneur but also a supermom and dedicated wife. She carved her successful journey by founding Real Estate SuperMoms, a unique venture that brings together her love for real estate and her passion for empowering women and mothers towards financial independence. When she's not closing deals or guiding fellow moms on investment strategies, you'll find Havan dedicatedly serving as Treasurer for the Vietnamese National Association of Real Estate Professionals, uplifting her community's involvement in the industry. Her life is a testament to her resilience, savvy business instincts, and an inspiring balance between professional accomplishments and cherished family moments.

RealEstateSuperMoms.com
PowerfulFemaleImmigrants.com